SKY HIGH PROFIT ROCKET

Edited by Roy Pellicano

EXPLOSIVE GROWTH FOR

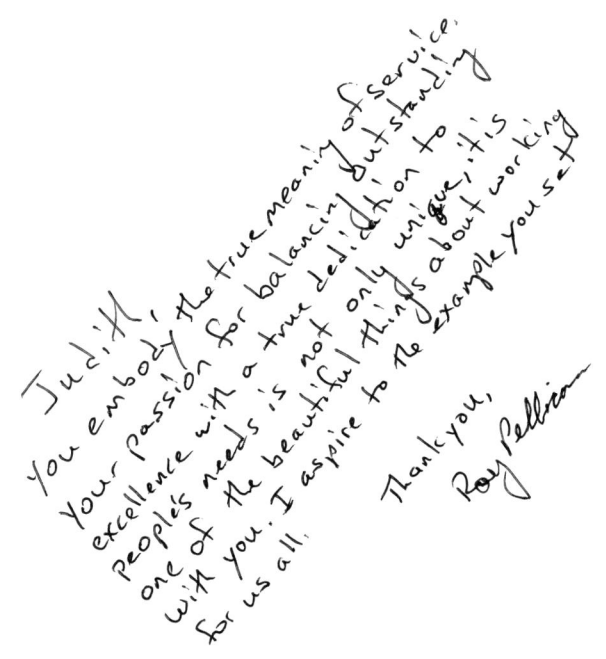

Judith,

You embody the true meaning of service. You passion for balancing outstanding excellence with a true dedication to people's needs is not only unique, it is one of the beautiful things about working with you. I aspire to the example you set for us all.

Thank you,
Roy Pellicano

YOUR BOTTOM LINE

AUTHOR'S SUMMARY

Business or product growth is predicated on many factors, including: Product Development; Brand Messaging; Sales Tactics; and Business Operations. This book provides practical tools and methods for anyone looking to grow a business, such as: product managers, sales people, business owners, executives, consultants, even employees who are looking to create "Me, Inc."

Three sections cover topics from Planning Your Business, Messaging Your Product, to Engaging Your Customer, including: case studies, tools to define a target market, systematizing workflows and process, creating powerful offers, actual sales letters to analyze, sales strategies, and entwining social proof into every aspect of the business.

To grow your business, you need to shift your thinking and you need practical and actual tools to achieve that growth. Sky High Profit Rocket is more than theory or instruction, it provides examples, tables, checklists, and processes to accomplish this. Plan to take notes!

COPYRIGHT AND DISCLAIMER

This material is copyrighted. No part, in whole or in part, may be reproduced by any process, or any other exclusive right exercised, without the permission of Tri-Angular Consulting, LLC © 2019

Roy Pellicano
Published by:
Tri-Angular Consulting, LLC
6830 Burns Street
Forest Hills, NY 11375
www.the-business-toolbox.com

DISCLAIMER AND/OR LEGAL NOTICES:

While every attempt has been made to verify information provided in this book, neither the editor nor the publisher assumes any responsibility for any errors, omissions or inaccuracies.

Any slights of people or organizations are unintentional. If advice concerning legal or related matters is needed, the services of a qualified professional should be sought. This book is not intended as a source of legal or accounting advice. You should be aware of any laws which govern business transactions or other business practices in your state or province.

The income statements and examples are not intended to represent or guarantee that everyone will achieve the same results. Individual success will be determined by his or her desire, dedication, effort, and motivation. There are no guarantees you will duplicate the results stated here, you recognize that any business endeavor has inherent risk for loss of capital.

Any reference to any persons or business, whether living or deceased, existing or defunct, is purely coincidental.

PRINTED IN USA

ISBN: 978-0-359-25458-3

DEDICATION

To all the small businesses owners
may your success be sky-high

To my family
may you always pursue your dreams
with all your heart

Roy

CONTENTS

PLANNING YOUR BUSINESS

Chapter 01	...	Leverage Marketing Case Studies	1
Chapter 02	...	Define Your Target Market	21
Chapter 03	...	Systemize Your Business and Develop Effective Processes	43
Chapter 04	...	Create Repeat Business: Have Clients that Pay, Stay and Refer	57

MESSAGING YOUR PRODUCT

Chapter 05	...	Create a Powerful Offer	65
Chapter 06	...	Risk Reversal to Increase Sales	73
Chapter 07	...	Create Profitable Sales Letters	83
Chapter 08	...	Profit Over the Phone	117

ENGAGING YOUR CUSTOMER

Chapter 9	...	Double your Referrals	133
Chapter 10	...	Use Testimonials and Profit from Social Proof	143

PERSONAL MESSAGE

My journey in supporting organizations has spanned more than 25 years and has included all sectors and sizes of business. My vision stems from a Systems orientation that was forged during my studies in Microbiology and Philosophy, and yet is grounded in concrete human-centric results, clear examples, and practical tools.

This book is a yet another step in my sharing and formalizing what I have learned about the foundational processes that can solve the basic need of every business owner: rocketing their profit so that it is sky-high.

$$\text{Customer's Wants} + \text{Needs} = \text{Your Customer's Problem}$$
$$\text{Customer's Problem} + \text{Your Solution} = \text{Your Revenue}$$
$$\text{Your Revenue} - \text{Your Costs} = \text{Your Profit}$$

Everything we do is tied to this equation, and that is as concrete as it can be. Increase your revenue by focusing on your customers' Wants, Needs, and Problems. Develop your message, hone your products, and decrease your costs by leveraging the tools, research, and knowledge provided herein.

Sky-High-Profit-Rocket is the first set of tools in The Business Toolbox

Roy

PS Enjoy the book and let me know how I can improve it in the future. www.The-Business-Toolbox.com

INTRODUCTION

Alzheimer's is a debilitating disease that destroys the mind and puts those who suffer from it in grave risk of harm. Facilities that care for these patients need to ensure that the patients do not "elope" from the care facilities.

To help staff, and not have a jail-like double locking door, there are elopement systems that are put in place around exit doors. At the time, the patients wore simple transmitters which set off an alarm if they came within the "no-go" zone. As the ramifications of elopement were severe, these systems were often tuned to be extra sensitive, thereby favoring false positives, and creating an environment of alarm-fatigue.

Using new cutting-edge technology, a company with which I worked created a product that would provide better precision with fewer false positives. Further the system could be implemented throughout the entire facility providing feedback in ways never before imagined.

Leadership were industry and technology professionals. With close to 100 years of experience between them they fully understood the operating environment and business needs of their target market. It was a great idea, a great product, and a great leadership team. Everything pointed to success and yet it failed because it was in fact a poor business.

The first indication that there was a serious problem with the business model pointed back to the product. Yes, it was expensive and installation was intrusive, but the partners were banking on the positives (including governmental reimbursement) to overcome these negatives.

What the leaders had failed to understand was what the market wanted was a much simpler product. After many failed attempts to achieve the precision we had sold to the customer, I apologized that we were just not going to achieve it in one particular area of the facility. The response was, "that is not a problem, we only need to know that they are in a room, not where they are in the room."

It took a lot of money and an overly complicated and expensive system to provide a product that was not really the needed solution. The company never recovered from that failure.

Measure twice (and then measure again) to ensure that you only cut once. If your idea is good, and the product is viable, and the business model looks to be a winner you will still fail if the market itself is not there. Focus on the basics: Wants, Needs, Problem, Solution. But if the market doesn't like the solution (or to rephrase it, if your solution is not the right solution) then you have no revenue and no opportunity to profit.

Marketing is not only about product positioning and branding, it is also about product development. This book is about marketing, but I want you to focus on the core aspects of product development, because no amount of marketing is going to help you sell a product with no perceived benefits.

Building a successful revenue model is based upon a successful product. Service businesses, such as an accountant or a dry cleaner, may consider themselves exempt from the discipline of Product Management, but if you consider your services to be individual (or even better, complementary) products you will be able to drive your profits sky-high.

Planning a successful business/product is predicated on the following four components: Product Development, Messaging, Sales Tactics, Product

Delivery. The dry cleaner may ask, "what kind of product development is there for me? I clean clothes using the products others have developed." This is the exact thinking that has crippled you and will continue to cripple your competitors. Change your thinking and you will be able to surpass them.

Your product is HOW you package and deliver your cleaning services using other people's products. For example, the cleaner that delivers and picks-up clothes; and provides real-time updates using text; and maybe even realizes that their customers may want additional services, say, to purchase specialty cleaning products or receive packages while away from home will achieve greater success than the dry cleaner that does not, if it is what the market wants.

A trick I like to use is to steal from other industries, business models, and technologies. Let's consider what can we learn from the eCommerce world to bring back to your business model. Maybe you can create a "platform," where you have "users" and you bundle services/products into a single eco-system thereby creating relevancy and drawing your customers in to purchase additional products from you.

Opening your mind to rethinking your business is what this book is about. I hope to provide you with Unique Insights that will Challenge your Assumptions and Change your Perspective.

The first five chapters will walk you through planning your product, which includes: looking at case studies (I love concrete examples); defining one's target market (always start with the customer); creating systems and formalizing you product/service delivery (this is your technology, even if you are not hi-tech); focusing on long-term success (by planning on how to continue to sell to your customers over time); and, positioning your products so that they will be irresistible to the consumer.

The next three chapters are about messaging, which includes: how to package your offer; how to craft a message that builds value; and, how to implement a sales letter--which can be used verbally in person, and over the phone.

The final three chapters are focused on generating repeat business (and building the foundation for enticing new customers) during the sales and delivery process, and discusses: how to leverage phone calls, referrals, and testimonials.

Plan to take notes as you go through the book--even if you already know a particular topic, there is value to reading the information again--even professional musicians practice their scales. The more notes you take as you are in the middle of the book, the better you will be positioned to actually use the methodologies outlined in this book.

1

Leverage From Marketing

Case Studies

The strategies discussed in this program mean absolutely nothing unless you choose to implement them.

The beauty of each of these time-tested strategies is that you can begin implementing them at any time – and start virtually anywhere in the program. There is no need to completely rework your entire marketing campaign or put off making changes until you can make all the changes at once.

This section profiles the success of others who have taken the information in this program and used it to better their businesses.

In each case, it took only a handful of changes to dramatically increase sales and generate higher revenues.

We start here so that you can let their stories motivate you to start working today to better your own business.

#	Business Type	Strategy	Marketing Materials
1	Professional Service	• Education	• Sales Script • Email Template • Workshop Invitation
2	Professional Service	• Intellectual Capital	• Sales Script • Referral Program
3	Professional Service	• Risk Reversal • Service Packaging	• Training Program • Sales Scripts • Loss Leader • Referral Program
4	Large-format	• Service Plan	• Product Collateral • Sales Script • Questionnaire
5	Professional Service	• Education • Expertise	• Expert Content • Free Seminars • Referral Program.
6	Professional Service	• Risk Reversal • Education	• Advertisements • Expert Content • Joint Ventures • Upsell • Loss Leader
7	Trade Service	• Competitor Research • Business Transformation	• Operations Manual • Marketing Manuals
8	Retail	• Joint Venture	• Direct Mail • Newspaper Ads • Joint Ventures
9	Restaurant (Retail)	• Target Market Research	• Personal Letters w/ Gift Certificates • Calendar of Events • New Brand Identity

#	Business Type	Strategy	Marketing Materials
10	Professional Service	• Risk Reversal • Powerful Offer	• Sales Letter • Sales Script • Referral Program
11	Professional Service	• Acquisition	• Sales Letter • Sales Script • Systemization • Sales Presentation
12	Professional Service	• Expert Positioning • SWOT Analysis	• Phone Script • Fax Flyers • Speakers Notes
13	Trade Service	• Aggressive Education	• Fundraising Program • Activities Program • Referral Program
14	Trade Service	• Value Added Packaging • Merchandising	• Point of sale Material • Magic Kits • Uniforms + T-Shirts • Referral Program • Sales Training
15	Professional Service	• Education • Expert Positioning • Intellectual Capital	• Sales Script • Referral Program • Process Systemization • Sales Letter
16	Trade Service	• Client Education • Service Program	• Staff Sales Script • Bonus Structure • Service Collateral

Case Study One

Think Coffee News

Business Type: Small Magazine Publisher (Professional Service)

Objective: Increase profits with cross selling opportunities, without any time expense.

Strategy: Education

Solution(s): A prominent marketing personality authored a regular column and a series of workshops to educate clients on easy-to-implement and cutting-edge marketing initiatives to sell clients a new twelve-month program.

Value Add Proposition: The twelve-month program would assist advertising clients on marketing their own business, creating better offers, back end sales, as well as profitable joint-venture opportunities.

Method: Free Series of Marketing Workshops + Newsletter Column

Marketing Materials:

- Sales Script to promote Starter Program
- Email Template
- Workshop Invitation

Result! A sustainable joint venture and cross selling opportunity was established and generates thousands of dollars in additional revenue per year.

Case Study Two

Young Realtor of the Year

Business Type: Independent Contractor (Professional Service)

Issue: Need to increase revenues, but has no extra time available after a successful marketing campaign.

Strategy: Intellectual Capital

Solution(s): When other local realtors phone for free advice, he sells them on shadowing him in action for a day, where they are free to take notes, and, guarantee they will not impede his ability to work nor talk to his clients.

Value Added Proposition: A one-hour debrief plus a handout highlighting the most important parts of day are included. A less successful realtor and inexperienced realtor is positioned as an expert and educated.

Method: Regular, time-consuming phone calls were turned into a source of revenue.

Marketing Materials:

- Sales Script
- Referral Program

Result! Realtor now makes $1,000 per day in addition to successful sales revenues with limited time investment.

Case Study Three

Personal Trainer

Business Type: Independent Contractor (Professional Service)

Objective: Generate more new leads and create a loyal client base

Strategy: Risk Reversal and Service Packaging

Solution(s): To understand why first-time buyers failed to purchase training, the first session was offered for free to clients who were qualified through a series of questions. This demonstrated credibility, empathy, insight, and most importantly the ability to provide a benefit to the person. Potential clients could evaluate the service before they opened their wallets.

Value Added Proposition: First session free, with package program of services available for $3,000 for Platinum clients.

Method: Advertise and promote free session

Marketing Materials:
- Training Program
- Sales Scripts
- Referral Program

Result! Personal Trainer tripled industry average revenues with this service package that sold for 10 times the industry average.

Case Study Four

Oil and Gas Company

Business Type: Large-format company

Objective: To increase annual transactions; most customers make 'one-time' purchases of large products that sell for approximately $70,000.

Strategy: Maintenance Program (Service Plan)

Solution(s): Machines seldom had any issues inside five years. A Warranty and Maintenance Program was developed to upsell each client and provide an opportunity to 'get in the door' of the customer quarterly.

Value Added Proposition: The $2,500 program was up-sold to each customer, providing an (almost) unconditional warranty and ease of mind.

Method: The serviceperson who made quarterly visits to each client also served as a salesperson looking for other opportunities

Marketing Materials:
- Collateral for other products
- Sales Script
- Questionnaire

Result! The 'lifetime value' of each client went up dramatically, and most sales were increased by $2,500 for the Maintenance Program.

Case Study Five

Accounting Company

Business Type: Professional Service

Objective: Need to grow business and increase revenues.

Strategy: Education and Expertise Positioning

Solution(s): Educate the market regarding tax strategies 'The Government Didn't Want You to Know'. Position the business as the experts with cutting edge advice and innovative money saving solutions for clients.

Value Added Proposition: Potential clients were able to gain 'free' information from the business, without making a purchase, which eliminates the risk involved in finding an accountant.

Method: Accountant wrote educational and informative tax columns as well as developed a regular string of seminars.

Marketing Materials:
- Newspaper + Newsletter Columns
- Free Seminars
- Referral Program.

Result! Firmly established themselves as the 'go to' company for businesses looking to pay less tax.

Case Study Six

Music Teacher

Business Type: Independent Contractor (Professional Service)

Objective: Need to generate more income to support ambitions

Strategy: Risk Reversal + Education

Solution(s): A two-hour adult group lesson. The most requested song was taught, and all were guaranteed to be able to play it. Clients were not interested in playing technically well, just to be able to play at Christmas, etc.

Value Added Proposition: Clients put no money down and would be an upsell of a 12-month training course to continue to develop their skills.

Method: Loss Leader was heavily promoted, and at the end of the session the students were sold a systematized 12-month training course.

Marketing Materials:
- SWOT Analysis
- Advertisements
- Newsletter
- Joint Ventures
- Upsell
- Loss Leader

Result! Licensed his program. He reckons he will have made more money off 'Unchained Melody' than the Righteous Brothers!

Case Study Seven

Lawn Mowing Business

Business Type: Professional Service (Trade)

Objective: Find a way to increase revenues and reduce overhead.

Strategy: Competitor Research and Business Transformation

Solution(s): Researched the five most successful businesses in their industry. Found the major competitors were companies selling 'licenses' rather than lawn services. Created everything to 'license' a business in a box.

Value Added Proposition: Offer $30,000.00 licenses, rather than $50 lawn mowing jobs.

Method: Took everything the company was doing successfully to operate a 'lawn mowing business' and completed manuals for operations and marketing based on existing systems.

Marketing Materials:

- Operations Manual
- Marketing Manuals

Result! Tripled previous year's sales with reduced overhead.

PLUS: Created frameworks for similar businesses and licensed these businesses.

Case Study Eight

Community Supermarket

Business Type: Product-based Business

Issue: Need to find a way to compete with other, larger, grocery stores and stop losing money.

Strategy: Joint Venture Marketing

Solution(s): Create a private label alternative with excellent branding and POS (point of sale) material. Joint venture with other small town supermarkets and ensured long term strategy to 'compete with big boys'.

Value Added Proposition: Huge increases in profit margin for an excellent product

Method: Full blown brand strategy.

Marketing Materials:
- Direct Mail
- Newspaper Ads
- Joint Ventures

Result! 22% increase in profitability.

Case Study Nine

Local Restaurant

Business Type: Service-based Business

Issue: Revenues in a downward spiral.

Strategy: Target Market Research

Solution(s): The clientele had changed but the restaurant was still operating based on what had worked in the past. The name was changed from 'Family Restaurant' to 'Pastaria'; younger staff were recruited; a calendar of events was created to draw crowds; and the brand identity was updated. The new image was one that their desired clientele would resonate with.

Value Added Proposition: Past influential customers were invited to try the revamped restaurant for free (through gift certificates).

Method: Personal letters were mailed to all popular and influential people in the local area.

Marketing Materials:
- Personal Letters including Gift Certificates
- Calendar of Events
- New Brand Identity

Result! Revenues tripled over twelve months.

Case Study Ten

Business Incubator

Business Type: Service-Based Business

Objective: Increase occupancy in short-term offices and increase profit.

Strategy: Risk Reversal; Powerful Offer

Solution(s): A powerful offer was created and targeted at small to medium sized business owners currently operating from home. The offer included minimal financial investment, ease of transition, and no commitment.

Value Added Proposition: New clients were offered their first month free, no deposit, no contract, and a free moving service. There was no risk for the client, and a powerful business operation environment was provided.

Method: Direct mail sales letter to potential clients operating from home, with follow up calls made by contract salespeople to close the sales.

Marketing Materials:

- Sales Letter
- Sale Script
- Referral Program.

Result! Doubled profits in first year and sustained growth.

Case Study Eleven

Business Incubator

Business Type: Service-Based Business

Objective: To grow the business after having doubled profits using their own system that increased occupancy by 22% above industry average.

Strategy: Purchase Competitors

Solution(s): Developed a list of competitors, and created a financial strategy to acquire them. Most jumped at the chance to exit the business as they were operating at industry average. Grew business and market share immediately and also created a viable option for someone looking to sell.

Value Added Proposition: The clients received superior service and were provided with greater leverage through the expanded service centers.

Method: Direct mail piece to all business centers offering to purchase.

Marketing Materials:
- Sales Letter
- Sales Script
- Systemization
- Sales Presentation

Result! Bought several of their competitors, increased market share and brand awareness substantially, profits grew by 75%.

Case Study Twelve

Mortgage Broker

Business Type: Independent Contractor (Professional Service)

Objective: Talented Mortgage Broker needs to grow clientele

Strategy: Expert Positioning

Solution(s): Increased Fees; customer Risk Reduction by establishing value and credentials prior to customers needing to commit.

Value Added Proposition: Potential customers received pressure free and cost-free information and expert advice before committing.

Method: Public speaking, free information nights and regular seminars/lunch and learns. Systemizing, recording and subsequently scripting initial consultations. She also leveraged an existing joint venture with very popular real estate office, and a ghost writer and licensed content.

Marketing Materials:
- Phone Script
- SWOT Analysis
- Fax Flyers
- Speakers Notes

Result! $27,245.00 profit in the first month as well as a successful business model that will be able to be licensed/sold.

Case Study Thirteen

Hockey Rink (in Australia!)

Business Type: Service-based Business (Trade Service)

Objective: Develop a school league for a sport that was not popular or well known in the Southern Hemisphere.

Strategy: Aggressive Education

Solution(s): Developed a skating program as lead generation and beginner hockey for those interested in trying the new sport. Becoming a school sport was difficult, but necessary for immediate and sustainable growth.

Value Added Proposition: Kids and parents were offered an alternative sport activity, and easier track to becoming an elite player.

Method: Created a school league using a grassroots campaign: the kids convinced parents, who in turn convinced teachers

Marketing Materials:
- Fundraising Program
- Activities Program
- Referral Program

Result! A school league with over 70 (paid) teams registered and state championships.

Case Study Fourteen

Magician

Business Type: Independent Contractor (Trade Service)

Objective: Make a profit!

Strategy: Value Added Packaging

Solution(s): A merchandise program supplemented revenue from regular magic shows: instead of donations at the end of each show (like most street performers), a salesperson was hired to man a table with t-shirts and magic kits, while the magician worked the crowd.

Value Added Proposition: Instead of a $5 donation, parents and kids could purchase $25 kits for home magic trick practice – a far better value.

Method: Table set up to sell merchandise; salesperson was hired.

Marketing Materials:
- Point of sale Material
- Magic Kits
- Uniforms + T-Shirts
- Referral Program
- Sales Training

Result! Tripled income immediately and was referred to larger paid gigs by audience members.

Case Study Fifteen

Magazine Publisher

Business Type: Independent Contractor (Professional Service)

Objective: To continue working after selling her business and being restricted by a 'non-compete' clause. She wanted to continue working.

Strategy: Education + Expert Positioning

Solution(s): Find a niche market using publishing expertise, and become a consultant, that trained other struggling publishing businesses on how to turn a handsome profit and avoid the common pitfalls of the business.

Value Added Proposition: Publishing businesses benefit from the expertise of a former competitor, without the high salary. The high profit but high failure industry of publishing has access to a proven success.

Method: Process formalization and sales letter followed by a phone call to all local publishing businesses.

Marketing Materials:

- Sales Script
- Referral Program
- Process Systemization
- Sales Letter

Result! She made more in this business than she did in the last!

Case Study Sixteen

Carpet Cleaning Company

Business Type: Service-based Business

Objective: Increase annual transactions and reduce acquisition cost.

Strategy: Client Education + Service Program

Solution(s): Most repeat clients clean carpets every 3-5 years. An education program centered around the health benefits of a cleaning frequency of every six months highlighted a health benefit over a health detriment.

Value Added Proposition: The six-month frequency would provide clients with a health benefit, instead of a health detriment.

Method: Educate sales team and train all staff on new scripts, then create marketing material to back up claims.

Marketing Materials:

- Staff Sales Script
- New Bonus Structure
- Service Collateral

Result! 27% (consistent with standard upselling statistics) of the clients bought into the program resulting in a HUGE increase in profitability.

2

Define Your Target Market

What is a Target Market?

Many businesses can't answer the question: *Who is your target market?* They have often made the fatal assumption that *everyone* will want to purchase their product or service with the right marketing strategy.

A target market is simply the group of customers or clients who will purchase a specific product or service. This group of people all have something in common, often age, gender, hobbies, or location.

Your target market, then, are the people who will buy your offering. This includes both existing and potential customers, all of whom are motivated to do one of three things:

- Fulfill a need
- Solve a problem
- Satisfy a desire

To build, maintain, and grow your business, you need to know who your customers are, what they do, what they like, and why they would buy your product or service. Getting this wrong – or not taking the time to get it right – will cost you time, money, and potentially the success of your business.

The Importance of Knowing Your Target Market

Knowledge and understanding of your target market is the keystone in the arch of your business. Without it, your product or service positioning, pricing, marketing strategy, and eventually, your business could very quickly fall apart.

If you don't intimately know your target market, you run the risk of making mistakes when it comes to establishing pricing, product mix, or service packages. Your marketing strategy will lack direction, and produce mediocre results at best. Even if your marketing message and unique selling proposition (USP) are clear, and your brochure is perfectly designed, it means nothing unless it arrives in the hands (or ears) of the right people.

Determining your target market takes time and careful diligence. While it often starts with a best guess, assumptions cannot be relied on and research is required to confirm original ideas. Your planned target market is not always your ideal market.

Once you build an understanding of who your target market is, keep up with your market research. Having your finger on the pulse of their motivations and drivers – which naturally change – will help you to anticipate needs or wants and evolve your business.

Types of Markets

Consumer

The Consumer Market includes those general consumers who buy products and services for personal use, or for use by family and friends. This is the market category you or I fall into when we're shopping for groceries or clothes, seeing a movie in the theatre, or going out for lunch. Retailers focus on this market category when marketing their goods or services.

Institutional

The Institutional Market serves society and provides products or services for the benefit of society. This includes hospitals, non-profit organizations, government organizations, schools and universities. Members of the Institutional Market purchase products to use in the provision of services to people in their care.

Business to Business (B2B)

The B2B Market is just what it seems to be: businesses that purchase the products and services of other business to run their operations. These purchases can include products that are used to manufacture other products (raw or technical), products that are needed for daily operations (such as office supplies), or services (such as accounting, shredding, and legal).

Reseller

This market can also be called the "Intermediary Market" because it consists of businesses that act as channels for goods and services between other markets. Goods are purchased and sold for a profit – without any alterations. Members of this market include wholesalers, retailers, resellers, and distributors.

Determining Your Target Market

Product / Service Investigation

The process for determining your target market starts by examining exactly what your offering is, and what the average customer's motivation for purchasing it is. Start by answering the questions on the next page:

Does your offering meet a basic need?	
Does your offering serve a particular want?	
Does your offering fulfill a desire?	
What is the lifecycle of your product / service?	
What is the availability of your offering?	
What is the cost of the average customer's purchase?	
What is the lifecycle of your offering?	
How many times or how often will customers purchase your offering?	
Do you foresee any upcoming changes in your industry or region that may affect the sale of your offering (positive/negative)?	

Market Investigation

On the ground. Spend some time on the ground researching who your target market might be. If you're thinking about opening a coffee shop, hang out in the neighborhood at different times of the day to get a sense of the people who live, work, and play in the neighborhood. Notice their age, gender, clothing, and any other indications of income and activities.

At the competition. Who is your direct competitor targeting? Is there a small niche that is being missed? Observing the clientele of your competition can help to build understanding of your target market, regardless of whether it is the same or opposite. For example, if you own a children's clothing boutique and the majority of middle-class mothers shop at the local department store, you may wish to focus on higher-income families as your target market.

Online. Many cities and towns – or at least regions – have demographic information available online. Research the ages, incomes, occupations, and other key pieces of information about the people who live in the area you operate your business. From this data, you will gain an understanding of the size of your total potential market.

With existing customers. Talk to your existing customers through focus groups or surveys. This is a great way to gather demographic and behavioral information, as well as genuine feedback about product or service quality and other information that will be useful in a business or marketing strategy.

Jobs That Need To Get Done

When we consider our target markets, traditionally we consider demographics and subsequently segment our customers: gender, age, race, social class, ethnicity, education level, etc. While there are valid reasons to think this way, we may want to consider segmentation, not by customer characteristic, but by the job they need to get done.

If your customer needs to have their dinner delivered to them right now, it may not matter if she is college educated, black, female, and Jewish. But it may matter that she needs it delivered in the next 30 minutes to feed her family because she was in a late meeting at the office and is now on the train home.

If the same customer is home alone with no external pressures, she may need a different service. Her need is not tied to her demographics, but the job she needs to get done. Offering her a speedy delivered family dinner at a premium, may not appeal to this need.

Who is Your Market?

Based on your product / service and market investigations, you will be able to piece together a basic picture of your target market, and some of their general characteristics. Record some notes here. At this point, you may wish to be as specific as possible, or maintain some generalities. You can further segment your market in the next section.

Differentiation as a Monopoly

Everything that I have described so far, and will continue to describe, throughout the rest of the book, is about driving differentiation. We don't think of differentiation as a monopoly, nor do we think of a monopoly as a critical part of marketing and business development, nevertheless, it is important to keep in mind in the context of targeting a market.

Traditionally, monopolies have been considered within the context of exclusion of other entities in a market. This is often accomplished through mergers and acquisitions and by growing so large you can dominate and compete unfairly. This is one way to think about a monopoly, but it is not what I mean, when I am describing "differentiation as a monopoly."

The most powerful type of monopoly comes from differentiating yourself and not from exclusion of others. Through true differentiation, you achieve monopoly simply through the fact that you ARE the only one providing a particular product. You compete against no one. This is all the more important in a commodity market. It is difficult to achieve but is worth the effort because the payoff is that valuable to your revenue growth.

Once you have a monopoly, you can then focus not on competing against others, but rather on driving success—just don't use it to harm your customers, like price gouging. Differentiate yourself, and you (and your customers) can focus on growth rather than focus on survival.

Consumer Target Market Framework

Market Type:	Consumer
Gender:	☐ Male ☐ Female
Age Range:	
Purchase Motivation:	☐ Meet a Need ☐ Serve a Want ☐ Fulfill a Desire
Activities:	
Income Range:	
Marital Status:	
Location:	☐ Neighborhood ☐ City ☐ Region ☐ Country
Jobs to Get Done:	
Other Notes:	

Institutional Target Market Framework

Market Type:	Institutional
Institution Type:	☐ Hospital ☐ Non-profit ☐ School ☐ University ☐ Charity ☐ Government ☐ Church
Purchase Motivation:	☐ Operational Need ☐ Client Want ☐ Client Desire
Purpose of Institution:	
Institution's Client Base:	
Size:	
Location:	☐ Neighborhood ☐ City ☐ Region ☐ Country
Jobs to Get Done:	
Other Notes:	

B2B Target Market Framework

Market Type:	Business to Business (B2B)
Company Size:	
Number of Employees:	
Purchase Motivation:	☐ Operations Need ☐ Strategy ☐ Functionality
Annual Revenue:	
Industry:	
Location(s):	
Purpose of Business:	
People, Culture, Values:	
Jobs to Get Done:	
Other Notes:	

Reseller Target Market Framework

Market Type:	Reseller
Industry:	
Client Base:	
Purchase Motivation:	☐ Operations Need ☐ Client Wants ☐ Functionality
Annual Revenue:	
Age:	
Location:	☐ Neighborhood ☐ City ☐ Region ☐ Country
Jobs to Get Done:	
Other Notes:	

Your Target Market: Putting It Together

Based on the information you gather from your product / service and market investigations, you should have a clear vision of your realistic target market. Here are a few examples of how this information is put together and conclusions are drawn:

Target Market Sample 1: Consumer Market

Business: Baby Clothing Boutique	**Business Purpose:** - *Meet a need* (provide clothing for infants and children aged 0 to 5 years) - *Serve a want* (clothing is brand name only, and has a higher price point than the competition)
Market Type: Consumer	
Gender: Women	
Marital Status: Married	
Market Observations: - located on Main Street of Anytown, a street that is seeing many new boutiques open up, proximate to the main shopping mall two blocks from popular mid-range restaurant that is busy at lunch	**Industry Predictions:** - large number of new housing developments in the city and surrounding areas - two new schools in construction - expect to see an influx of new families move to town from Anycity
Competition Observations: - baby clothing also available at two local department stores, and one second-hand shop on opposite side of town	**Online Research:** - half of Anytown's population is female, and 25% have children under the age of 15 years - Anytown's population is expected to increase by 32% within three years - the average household income for Anytown is $75,000 annually

TARGET MARKET:

The target market can then be described as married mothers with children under five years old, between the ages of 25 and 45, who have recently moved to Anytown from Anycity, and have a household income of at least $100k annually.

Target Market Sample 2: B2B Market

Business: Confidential Paper Shredding	**Target Business Size:** Small to medium
Market Type: B2B (Business to Business)	**Target Business Revenue:** $500K to $1M
Business Purpose: - *Meet an operations need* (provide confidential on-site shredding services for business documents)	**Target Business Type:** - produce or handle a variety of sensitive paper documentation - accountants, lawyers, real estate agents, etc.
Market Observations: - there are two main areas of office buildings and industrial warehouses in Anycity - three more office towers are being constructed, and will be completed this year	**Industry Predictions:** - the professional sector is seeing revenue growth of 24% over last year, which indicates increased client billing and staff recruitment
Competition Observations: - one confidential shredding company serves the region, covering Anycity and the surrounding towns - provide regular (weekly or biweekly) service, but does not have the capacity to handle large volumes at one time	**Online Research:** - Anycity's biggest employment sectors are: manufacturing, tourism, food services, and professional services
TARGET MARKET: *The target market can then be described as small to medium sized businesses in the professional sector with an annual revenue of $500K to $1M who require both regular and infrequent large volume paper shredding services.*	

Segmenting Your Market

Your market segments are the groups within your target market – broken down by a determinant in one of the following four categories:

- Demographics
- Psychographics
- Geographics
- Behaviors

Segmenting your target market into several more specific groups allows you to further tailor your marketing campaign and more specifically position your product or service. Earlier we spoke about the Jobs that People Need to Get Done, and this is another way to segment your market.

Don't get too crazy with segmentation but choose the characteristics that are truly differentiating, achievable, real, and measurable. You may wish to divide your ad campaign into four sections, and target four specific markets with messages that will most resonate with the audience.

For example, the baby clothing store may segment its target market by lifestyle or psychographics. If the larger target market is *married females with children under five, between the ages of 25 and 45, who have a household income of at least $100K annually*, it can be broken down into the following segments:

- Fitness-oriented mothers
- Career-oriented mothers
- New mothers

With these three categories, unique marketing messages can be created that speak to the hot-buttons of each segment. The more accurate and specific you can make communications with your target market, the greater impact you will have on your revenues.

Market Segmentation Variables

Demographic	*Psychographic*	*Geographic*	*Behavioristic*
Age Income Gender Generation Nationality Ethnicity Marital Status Family Size Occupation Religion Language Education Employment Type Housing Type Housing Ownership Political Affiliation	Personality Lifestyle Values Attitude Motivation Activities Interests	Region Country City Area Neighborhood Density Climate	Brand Loyalty Product Usage Purchase Frequency Profitability Readiness to Buy User Status

Understanding Your Target Market

Once you have determined who your market is, make a point of learning everything you can about them. You need to have a strong understanding of who they are, what they like, where they shop, why they buy, and how they spend their time. Remind yourself that you may *think* you know your market, but until you have verified the information, you'll be driving your business blind.

Also, be aware that markets change, just like people. Just because you knew your market when you started your business 10 years ago, doesn't mean you know it now. Regular market research is part of any successful business plan, and a great habit to start.

Types of Market Research

SURVEY

The simplest way to gather information from your clients or target market is through a survey. You can craft a questionnaire full of questions about your product, service, market demographics, buyer motivations, and so on. Plus, anonymous surveys will produce the most accurate information since names are not attached to the results or specific comments.

Depending on the purpose—whether it is to gather demographic information, product or service feedback, or other data—there are a number of ways to administer a survey.

TELEPHONE

Telephone surveys are a more time-consuming option, but have the benefit of live communication with your target market. Generally, it is best to have a third party conduct this type of survey to gather the most honest feedback. This is the method that market researchers use for polling, which is highly reliable.

ONLINE

Online surveys are the easiest to administer yourself. There a many web-based services that quickly and easily allow you to custom create your survey, and send it to your email marketing list. These services can also analyze, summarize and interpret the results on your behalf. Keep in mind that the results include only those who are motivated to respond, which may slant your results.

PAPER-BASED

Paper surveys are seldom used and can prove to be an inefficient method. Like online surveys, your results are based on the feedback of those who were motivated for one reason or another to respond. However, the time and effort involved in taking the survey, filing it out, and returning it to your place of business may deter people from participating.

DURING SALE

Every sale interaction is a time to elicit feedback to ensure relevancy and drive home the point that you care about your customer. A simple question after the sale can not only deliver insight, but also engender ownership on the part of your customer: "Is there anything we could do to make this better?"

Keep in mind that surveys can be complex to administer and consume more time and resources than you have planned. If you have the budget, consider hiring a professional market research firm to lead or assist with the process. This will also ensure that the methodology is standard practice and will garner the most accurate results.

Website Analysis

Tracking your website traffic is an excellent way to research your existing and potential customer's interests and behavior. From this information, you can ensure the design, structure and content of your website is catering to the people who use it – and the people you want to use it.

User-friendly website traffic analytics programs can easily show you who is visiting your site, where they are from, and what pages of your site they are viewing. Services like Google Analytics can tell you what page they arrive at, where they click to, how much time they spend on each page, and on which page they leave the site.

This is powerful (and free!) information to have in your market research, and easy to monitor monthly or weekly, depending on the needs of your business. Be careful though, this analysis is used to assume intent from behavior, and always remember that you must validate any analysis that comes from deciphering intent or benefit from behavior.

Customer Purchase Data (Consumer Behavior)

If you do not have the budget to conduct your own professional market research, you can use existing resources on consumer behavior. While this data may not be specific to your region or city, general consumer research is actual data that can be helpful in confirming assumptions you may have made about your target market.

Your customer loyalty program or Point of Sale system may also be of help in tracking customer purchases and identifying trends in purchase behavior. If you can track who is buying, what they're buying and how often they're buying, you'll have an arsenal of powerful insight into your existing client base.

Focus Groups

Focus groups look at the psychographic and behavioristic aspects of your target market and are good at identifying Jobs that Need to Get Done, Needs, and Wants. Further, the insights can be leveraged outside of the specific Focus Group dynamic to build larger insight into growth areas not currently in your view.

Groups of six to 12 people are gathered and asked general and specific questions about their purchase motivations and behaviors. These questions could relate to your business, in particular, or to the general industry.

Focus group sessions can also be time consuming to organize and facilitate, so consider hiring the services of a professional market research firm. You may also receive more honest information if a third party is asking the questions and receiving the responses from focus group participants.

For cost savings, consider partnering with an associate in the same industry who is not a direct competitor, and who would benefit from the same market data.

3

Systemizing Your Business and Developing Effective Processes

One of the biggest mistakes a business owner can make is to create a company that is dependent on the owner's involvement for the success of its daily operations. This is called working "in" your business. You're writing basic sales letters, licking stamps, and guiding staff step-by-step through each task.

There are a number of problems with this approach. One is redundancy. You're paying your staff to carry out tasks that you eventually complete. The second is poor time management. You're spending your day – at your high hourly rate – on tasks as they arise, leaving little room for the tasks you need to be focused on.

However, the biggest issue I have with this approach is that countless intelligent business owners are spending the majority of their time operating their business, instead of *growing* it.

A good test of this is to ask yourself, what would happen if you took off to a hot sunny destination for three weeks and left your cell phone, PDA and laptop at home. Would your business be able to continue operating?

If you said no, then this chapter is for you.

Systemizing your business is about putting policies and procedures in place to make your business operations run smoother – and more importantly – without your constant involvement. With your newfound free time, **you will be able to focus your efforts on the bigger picture: strategically growing your business.**

Why Systemize?

For most small business owners, systems simply mean freedom from the day-to-day functioning of their organization. The company runs smoothly, makes a profit, and provides a high level of service – regardless of the owner's involvement.

Systemizing your business is also a healthy way to plan for the future. You're not going to be working forever – what happens when you retire? How will you transition your business to new ownership or management? How will you take that vacation you've been dreaming of?

Businesses that function without their ownership are also highly valuable to investors. Systemizing your business can position it in a favorable light for purchase and merit a high price tag. Further, systemization can become the means to developing a new line of revenue, in and of itself.

A system is any process, policy, or procedure that consistently achieves the same result, regardless of who is completing the task.

Any task that is performed in your business more than once can be systemized. Ideally, the tasks that are completed on a cyclical basis – daily, weekly, monthly, and quarterly – should be systemized so much so that anyone can perform them.

Systems can take many forms – from manuals and instruction sheets, to signs, banners, and audio or video recordings. They don't have to be elaborate or extensive, just provide enough information in step-by-step form to guide the person performing the task.

While the term "technology" is generally used to refer to computers, the internet, mobile apps, social media, and the like, it has a more traditional and formal meaning. The systemization that I am describing is included in that traditional definition of technology, and just like any other technology, it is how you can drive growth.

If you review the Case Studies in Chapter 1, you will see how systemization changed and created exponential opportunities of growth for those businesses. This technology created exponential growth opportunities for the businesses that created and implemented it.

Benefits of Business Systems

There are unlimited benefits available to you and your business through systemization. The more systems you can successfully implement, the more benefits you'll see.

- Better cost management
- Improved time management
- Clearer expectations of staff
- More effective staff training and orientation
- Increased productivity (and potentially profits)
- Happier customers (consistent service)
- Maximized conversion rates
- Increased staff respect for your time
- Increased level of individual initiative
- Greater focus on long-term business growth

Taking Stock of Your Existing Systems

The first step in systemizing your business is taking a long look at the existing systems (if any) in your business. At this point, you can look for any systems that have simply emerged as "the way we do things here."

How do your staff answer the phone? What is the process customers go through when dealing with your business? How are employees hired? Trained? How is performance Reviewed and rewarded?

Some of your systems may be highly effective, and not require any changes. Others may be ineffective and require some reworking. If you have previously established some systems, now is a good time to check-in and evaluate how well they are functioning.

Use the following chart to record what systems currently exist in your business.

Existing Systems	
Administration	
Financials	
Communication	
Customer Relations	
Employees	
Marketing	
Data	

Seven Areas to Systemize

There is no doubt that system creation – especially when none exist to begin with – is a daunting and time-consuming task. For many businesses, it can be difficult to determine where to start to make the best use of their time from the onset.

Here are seven main areas of your business you can to systemize. Begin with one area and move to the other areas as you are ready. Alternately, start with one or two systems within each area, and evaluate how those new systems affect your business. Each business will require its own unique set of systems.

1. Administration

This is an important area of your business to systemize because administrative roles tend to see a high turnover. A series of systems will reduce training time and keep you from explaining how the phones are to be answered each time a new receptionist joins your team.

Administrative Systems	
Opening and closing procedures	Filing and paper management
Phone greeting	Workflow
Mail processing	Document production
Sending couriers	Inventory management
Office maintenance (watering plants, emptying recycle bins, etc.)	Order processing
	Making orders

2. Financials

This is one area of systems that you will need to keep a close eye on – but that doesn't mean you have to do the work yourself. Financial management systems are everything from tracking credit card purchases to invoicing clients and following up on overdue accounts.

These systems will help to prevent employee theft and allow you to always have a clear picture of your numbers. It will allow you to control purchasing and ensure that each decision is signed-off on.

Financial Systems	
Purchasing	Profit / loss statements
Credit card purchase tracking	Invoicing
Accounts payable	Daily cash out
Accounts receivable	Petty cash
Bank deposits	Employee expenses
Cutting checks	Payroll
Tax payments	Commission payments

3. Communications

The area of communication is essential and time consuming for any business. Fax cover letters, sales letters, internal memos, reports, and newsletters are items that need to be created regularly by different people in your organization.

Most of the time, these communications aren't much different from one to the next, yet each are created from scratch by a different person. There is a huge opportunity for systemization in this area of your business. Systemized communication ensures consistency and company differentiation.

Communication Systems	
Internal memo template	Newsletter template
Fax cover template	Sales letter template(s)
Letterhead template	Meeting minutes template
Team meeting agenda	Report template
Sending faxes	Internal meetings
Internal emails	Scheduling

4. Customer Relations

Another important area for systemization is customer relations. This includes everything the customer sees or touches in your company, as well as any interaction they might have with you or your staff members.

Establishing a customer relations system will also ensure that new staff members understand how customers are handled in *your* business. It will allow you to maintain a high level of customer service, without constantly reminding staff of your policies. It will also ensure that the success of your customer relations and retention does not hinge on you or any other individual salesperson.

Customer Relations Systems	
Incoming phone call script	Sales process
Outgoing phone call script	Sales script
Customer service standards	Newsletter templates
Customer retention strategy	Ongoing customer communication strategy
Customer communications templates	Customer liaison policy

5. Employees

Create systems in your business for hiring, training, and developing your employees. This will establish clear expectations for the employee, and streamline time consuming activities like recruitment.

Employees with clear expectations who work within clear structures are happier and more productive. They are motivated to achieve 'A' when they know they will receive 'B' if they do. Establishing a clear training manual will also save you and your staff the time and hassle of training each new staff member on the fly.

Employee Systems	
Employee recruitment Employee retention Incentive and rewards program Regular employee reviews Employee feedback structure	Staff uniforms or dress code Employee training Ongoing training and professional development Job descriptions and role profiles

6. Marketing

This is likely an area in which you spend a large part of your time. You focus on generating new leads and getting more people to call you or walk through your doors. These efforts can be systemized and delegated to other staff members.

Use the information in this program to create simple systems for your basic promotional efforts. Any one of your staff should be able to pick up a marketing manual and implement a successful direct mail campaign or place a purposeful advertisement.

Marketing Systems	
Referral program	Regular advertisements
Customer retention program	Advertisement creation system
Regular promotions	Direct mail system
Marketing calendar	Sales procedures
Enquiries management	Lead management

7. Data

While we like to think we operate a paperless office, often the opposite is true. Your business needs to have clear systems for managing paper and electronic information to ensure that information is protected, easily accessed, and only kept when necessary.

Data management systems help you keep your office organized. Everyone knows where information is to be stored, and how it is to be handled, which prevents big stacks of paper with no place to go.

Ensure that within your data management systems you include a data backup system. That way, if anything happens to you server or computer software, your data – and potentially your business – is protected.

Data Management Systems	
IT Management	Client file system
Data backup	Project file system
Computer repairs	Point of sale system
Electronic information storage	Financial data management

Implementing New Systems

If you completed the exercise earlier in this chapter, you will have a good idea of the systems that are currently in place in your business. The next step is to determine what systems you need to create in your business.

To do this you will need to get a better understanding of the tasks that you and your employees complete on a daily and weekly basis. If you operate a timesheet program, this can be a good source of information. Alternately, ask staff to keep a daily log for a week of all the tasks they contribute to or complete. Doing so will not only give you valuable insight into their how they spend their time on a daily basis, but also involve them in the systemizing process.

Review all task logs or timesheet records at the end of the week, remove duplicates, and group like tasks together. From here you can categorize the tasks into business areas like the seven listed above or create your own categories.

Then, you will need to prioritize and plan your system creation and implementation efforts. Choose one from each category, or one category to focus on at a time. The amount you can take on will depend on your business needs, and the staff resources you have available to you for this process.

Remember that system creation is a long-term process – not something that will transform your business overnight. Be patient, and focus on the items that hold the highest priority.

Creating Your Systems

There is a big variety of ways you can create systems for your business – depending on the type of system you need and the type of business you operate. Some systems will be short and simple – i.e., a laminated sign in the kitchen that outlines step-by-step how to make the coffee – while others will be more complex – i.e., your sales scripts or letter templates.

One thing all of your systems have in common is steps. There is a linear process involved from start to finish. Begin by writing out each of the steps involved in completing the task and provide as much detail as you can.

Then, review your step-by-step guide with the employee(s) who regularly complete the task and gather their feedback. Once you have incorporated their input, decide what format the system needs to be in: manual, laminated instruction sheet, sign, office memo, etc.

Testing Your Systems

Now that you have created a system, you will need to make sure that it works. More specifically, you need to make sure that it works without your involvement.

Implement the new system for an appropriate period of time – a week or month – then ask for input from staff, suppliers and vendors, and customers. Evaluate if it is informative enough for your staff, seamless enough for your suppliers, and whether or not it meets or exceeds your customer's needs.

Take that feedback and revise the system accordingly. You will rarely get the system right the first time – so be patient.

Systems will also need to be evaluated and revised on a regular basis to ensure your business processes are kept up to date. Structure an annual or bi-annual review of systems and stick to it.

Employee Buy-In

It will be nearly impossible for you to develop effective systems without the involvement and input of your employees. These are the people who will be using the systems, and who are completing the tasks on a regular basis without systems. They have a wealth of knowledge to assist you in this process.

Employees can also draft the systems for you to review and finalize. This will make the systemization process a much faster and more efficient one.

It is also important to note that when you introduce new systems into your company, there may be a natural resistance to the change. People – including your employees – are habitual people who can become set in the way they are used to doing things.

Delegation

The final step to systemizing your business is delegation. What is the point of creating systems unless someone other than you can use them to perform tasks?

This doesn't have to mean completely removing your involvement from the process, but it does mean giving your employees enough freedom to complete the task within the structure of the systems you have spent time and considerable thought creating.

After that, allow yourself the freedom of focusing on the tasks that you most enjoy, and most deserve your time – like creating big picture strategies to grow your business and increase your profits.

4

Create Repeat Business:

Have Clients that Pay, Stay and Refer

When it comes to marketing and generating more income, most business owners are focused outward.

They've carefully established and segmented their target market and created specific offers and messages for each market segment. They spend thousands of dollars in advertising and direct mail campaigns in hot pursuit of more leads, more customers, and more foot traffic.

While this is an effective way to build a business, it is costly and time consuming. It requires constant and consistent effort, and while this approach does generate results, those results quickly disappear when the effort stops or becomes less intense.

Successful businesses that see sustained growth have a double-edged marketing strategy. They focus their efforts *outward* – on new potential customers and marketing – as well as *inward* – on existing customers and referral business.

These successful businesses have leveraged their existing efforts to generate more revenue. Simply put, their customers buy from them over and over again.

For most businesses, this is the easiest way to increase their revenues. Simple customer loyalty strategies and outstanding customer service are often all you need to dramatically increase your sales – from the customers you already have.

The Cost of Your Customers

Do you know how much it costs your business to buy new customers?
Each new customer that walks through your door – with the exception of referrals – has cost you money to acquire. You have spent money on advertising and promotions to generate leads and turn those leads into customers.

For example, if you have placed an ad in your local newspaper for $1,000, and the ad brings in 10 customers, you have paid $100 to acquire each customer. You would need to ensure each of those customers spent at least $200 to cover your margin and break even.

Alternately, if you spent two hours of your time and $10 per month on an email marketing program to send a newsletter to your existing database of customers, and you bring in 10 customers as a result – each customer has cost you $1.

Generating more repeat business means focusing on the marketing strategies that aim to keep your existing customers instead of purchase new ones – effectively reducing the cost of attracting new customers to your business.

These strategies are simple to implement, and don't require much time investment. Just a solid understanding of how to make customers want to come back and spend more of their money

Keeping Your Customers

Marketing strategies that focus on keeping your current customer base are easy and enjoyable to implement. They allow you to build real relationships with the people you do business with, instead of dealing with a revolving door of people on the other end of your sales process.

Repeat customers create a community of people around your business that presumably share the same needs, desires and frustrations. The information you gain from these customers (market research) can help you strengthen your understanding of your target audience, and more accurately segment it.

Remember – 80% of your revenue comes from 20% of your customers. Always focus on these customers. They are ideal customers that you want to recruit and hold on to.

Customer Service: Make them love buying from you

Every business – even those with excellent service standards can improve the service they provide their customers. Customer service seems to be a dying concept in most businesses; more focus seems to be placed on the speed of the transaction. These days you can even go to the grocery store now and not speak to a single sales associate thanks to self-serve checkouts.

To improve your company's customer service standards, take a survey of your customers and your employees to brainstorm ways you can improve the experience of buying from your business.

Successful customer service standards – those that make your customers *buy* – are:

Consistent. The standards are up kept by every person in your organization. Expectations are clear and followed through. Customers know what to expect and choose your business because of those expectations.

Convenient. It is nearly effortless for the customer to spend money at your place of business. Convenience can take many forms – location, product selection, value-added services like delivery – and it is also consistent.

Customer-driven. The service the customer receives is exactly how they would like to be treated when buying your product or service. It is reflective of your target market, and appropriate to their lifestyle. Customers would probably not appreciate white linen tablecloths at a fast food restaurant, but they would appreciate a 2-minutes or less guarantee.

Newsletters: Keep in touch with your customers

A regular newsletter is an easy, time-effective, and inexpensive marketing strategy to implement. Unfortunately, many small businesses think these are too time consuming and too expensive to adopt as part of their marketing strategy.

The most popular type of newsletter distribution is email. This will cost your business as little at $10 per month for an email marketing service subscription and can be customized to your unique branding.

Here is an easy five-step process to starting a company newsletter:

1. **Pick your audience.** New customers? Market segment? Existing customers?
2. **Choose what you're going to say.** Company news? Feature product? New offer?
3. **Determine how you're going to say it.** Articles? Bullet points? Pictures?
4. **Decide how it's going to get to your audience.** Email? Mail? In-store?
5. **Track your results.** How many people opened it? Read it? Took action?

Value Added Service: Give them happy surprises

Adding value to your business is an effective way of getting your customers back. Every person I know would choose a mattress store that offered free delivery over one that did not. It's that simple.

There are many ways to add value to your business, including:

- **Feature your expertise.** Use your knowledge to provide additional value to your customers. Offer a free consumer guide or report with every purchase.

- **Add convenience services.** Offer a service that makes their purchase easier, or more convenient. The best example of this is free shipping or delivery.
- **Package complementary services.** Packaging like items together creates an increase in perceived value. This is great for start-up kits.
- **Offer new products or services.** Feature top of the line or exclusive products, available only at your business. Offer a new service or profile a new staff member with niche expertise.

Value added services generate repeat customers in one of two ways:

1. Impress them on their first visit. Impress you customer with great service, a product that meets their needs, and then wow them with something extra that they weren't expecting. Get them to associate the experience of dealing with your business with happy surprises and create a perception of higher value.

2. Entice them to come back. The introduction of a new value-added service can be enough to convince a customer to buy from you again. Their initial purchase established a trust and knowledge of your business and its processes. They will want to "be included" in anything new you have to offer – especially if there is exclusivity. It is easier to attract clients that have purchased from you than potential clients who have not.

3.Customer Loyalty Programs: Give them incentives

Another simple way to keep in touch with existing customers and keep them coming back to you is to create a customer loyalty program. Successful loyalty programs are about fostering stakeholder engagement. These are serious programs that need to be contemplated and implemented as a critical part of the customer experience.

A "bolt-on" implementation will never be as successful as one where the engagement experience is tightly coupled to the value proposition that has been developed for each individual product.

These programs do not have to be complicated or costly and are relatively easy to maintain once they have been implemented. These programs help you gain more information on your customers and their purchasing habits.

Here are some examples of simple loyalty programs that you can implement:

- **Free product or service.** Give them every 10th (or 6th) product or service free. Produce stamp cards with your logo and contact information on it.

- **Reward dollars.** Give them a certain percentage of their purchase back in money that can only be spent in-store. Produce "funny money" with your logo and brand.

- **Rewards points.** Give them a certain number of points for every dollar they spend. These points can be spent in-store, or on special items you bring in for points only.

- **Membership amenities.** Give members access to VIP amenities that are not available to other customers. Produce member cards or give out member numbers.

Remember that in order for this strategy to work, you and your team have to understand and promote it. The program in and of itself becomes a product that you sell. Its purpose is to support engagement.

5

Create a Powerful Offer

I'm not going to beat around the bush on this one:

Your offer is the granite foundation of your business.

Get it right, and everything else will fall into place. Your headline will grab readers, your copy will sing, your ad layout will hardly matter, and you will have customers running to your door.

Get it wrong, and even the best looking, best-written campaign will sink like the Titanic.

A powerful offer is an irresistible offer. It's an offer that gets your audience frothing at the mouth and clamoring over each other all the way to your door. An offer that makes your readers pick up the phone and open their wallets.

Irresistible offers make your potential customers think, "I'd be crazy not to take him up on that," or "An offer like this doesn't come around very often." They instill a sense of emotion, of desire, and ultimately, urgency.

Make it easy for customers to purchase from you the first time, and spend your time keeping them coming back.

I'll say it again: **get it right, and everything else will fall into place.** For this reason, the offer needs to be tightly integrated with your business model, your product offering, and your overall market strategy.

The Crux of Your Marketing Campaign

As you work your way through this program, you will find that nearly every chapter discusses the importance of a powerful offer as related to your marketing strategy or promotional campaign.

There's a reason for this. The powerful offer is more often than not the reason a customer will open their wallets. It is how you generate leads, and then convert them into loyal customers. The more dramatic, unbelievable, and valuable the offer is the more dramatic and unbelievable the response will be.

Many companies spend thousands of dollars on impressive marketing campaigns in glossy magazines and big city newspapers. They send massive direct mail campaigns on a regular basis; yet don't receive an impressive or massive response rate.

These companies do not yet understand that simply providing information on their company and the benefits of their product is not enough to get customers to act. There is no reason to pick up the phone or visit the store, *right now*.

Your powerful, irresistible offer can:

- Increase leads
- Drive traffic to your website or business
- Move old product

- Convert leads into customers
- Build your customer database

What Makes a Powerful Offer?

A powerful offer is one that makes the most people respond, and take action. It gets people running to spend money on your product or service.

Powerful offers nearly always have an element of *urgency* and of *scarcity*. They give your audience a reason to act immediately, instead of putting it off until a later date.

Urgency relates to time. The offer is only available until a certain date, during a certain period of the day, or if you act within a few hours of seeing the ad. The customer needs to act now to take advantage of the offer.

Scarcity relates to quantity. There are only a certain number of customers who will be able to take advantage of the offer. There may be a limited number of spaces, a limited number of products, or simply a limited number of people the business will provide the offer to. Again, this requires that the customer acts immediately to reap the high value for low cost.

Powerful offers also:

Offer great value. Customers perceive the offer as having great value – more than a single product on its own, or the product at its regular price. It is clear that the offer takes the reader's needs and wants into consideration.

Make sense to the reader. They are simple and easy to understand if read quickly. Avoid percentages – use half off or 2 for 1 instead of 50% off. There are no "catches" or requirements; no fine print.

Seem logical. The offer doesn't come out of thin air. There is a logical reason behind it – a holiday, end of season, anniversary celebration, or new product. People can get suspicious of offers that seem "too good to be true" and have no apparent purpose.

Provide a premium. The offer provides something extra to the customer, like a free gift, or free product or service. They feel they are getting something extra for no extra cost. Premiums are perceived to have more value than discounts.

Remember that when your target market reads your offer, they will be asking the following questions:

1. What are you offering me?
2. What's in it for me?
3. What makes me sure I can believe you?
4. How much do I have to pay for it?

The Most Powerful Types of Offers

Decide what kind of offer will most effectively achieve your objectives. Are you trying to generate leads, convert customers, build a database, move old product off the shelves, or increase sales?

Consider what type of offer will be of most value to your ideal customers – what offer will make them act quickly.

Free Offer

This type of offer asks customers to act immediately in exchange for something free. This is a good strategy to use to build a customer database or mailing list. Offer a free consultation, free consumer report, or other item of low cost to you but of high perceived value.

You can also advertise the value of the item you are offering for free. For example, act now and you'll receive a free consultation, worth $75 dollars. This will dramatically increase your lead generation and allow you to focus on conversion when the customer comes through the door or picks up the phone.

The Value-Added Offer

Add additional services or products that cost you very little and combine them with other items to increase their attractiveness. This increases the perception of value in the customer's mind, which will justify increasing the price of a product or service without incurring extra hard costs to your business.

Package Offer

Package your products or services together in a logical way to increase the perceived value as a whole. Discount the value of the package by a small margin and position it as a "start-up kit" or "special package." By packaging goods of mixed values, you will be able to close more high-value sales. For example: including a free desk-jet printer with every computer purchase.

Premium Offer

Offer a bonus product or service with the purchase of another. This strategy will serve your bottom line much better than discounting. This includes 2 for 1 offers, offers that include free gifts, and in-store credit with purchases over a specific dollar amount.

Urgency Offer

As I mentioned above, offers that include an element of urgency enjoy a better response rate, as there is a reason for your customers to act immediately. Give the offer a deadline or limit the number of spots available.

Guarantee Offer

Offer to take the risk of making a purchase away from your customers. Guarantee the performance or results of your product or service and offer to compensate the customer with their money back if they are not satisfied. This will help overcome any fear or reservations about your product and make it more likely for your leads to become customers.

Create Your Powerful Offer

Pick a single product or service.
Focus on only one product or service – or one product or service *type* – at a time. This will keep your offer clear, simple, and easy to understand. This can be an area of your business you wish to grow, or old product that you need to move off the shelves.

Decide what you want your customers to do.

What are you looking to achieve from your offer? If it is to generate more leads, then you'll need your customer to contact you. If it is to quickly sell old product, you'll need your customer to come into the store and buy it. Do you want them to visit your website? Sign up for your newsletter? How long do they have to act? Be clear about your call to action, and state it clearly in your offer.

Dream up the biggest, best offer.

First, think of the biggest, best things you could offer your customers – regardless of cost and ability. Don't limit yourself to a single type of offer, combine several types of offers to increase value. Offer a premium, plus a guarantee, with a package offer. Then take a look at what you've created and make the necessary changes so it is realistic.

Run the numbers.

Finally, make sure the offer will leave you with some profit – or at least allow you to break even. You don't want to publish an outrageous offer that will generate a tremendous number of leads, but leave you broke. Remember that each customer has an acquisition cost, as well as a lifetime value. The amount of their first purchase may allow you to break even, but the amount of their subsequent purchases may make you a lovely profit.

6

Risk Reversal to Increase Sales

What is the biggest objection you need to overcome when closing a sale? Is it cost? Belief in what you have to say? Confidence in your product or service?

While it is a different answer for every business, every business has to deal with some element of customer fear or hesitation before a monetary transaction.

The reality is that even if you overcome these objections and close the sale, your customer walks away carrying 99% of the risk associated with the purchase. If the product doesn't work, breaks down, or doesn't perform to expectations, your customer has parted with their dollars in exchange for disappointment.

In marketing, one objective is to generate as many leads as possible, then to convert each lead into a customer, or sale. The ratio of leads to closed sales is called your conversion rate.

What if you could eliminate the risk involved in a transaction? Would you turn more leads into customers? The answer is absolutely.

Introducing a risk reversal element into your marketing message or unique offer is a powerful way to give yourself an edge on the competition and close more sales. But how exactly are you going to do this?

It's easy – just give them a guarantee.

The Power of Guarantees

What is Risk Reversal?

Risk reversal simply refers to reversing the risk associated with a transaction – transferring it from the customer to the vendor.

Everyone can think of a handful of times they have purchased a product or service that did not deliver on their expectations. A time where a salesperson made them a promise and did not deliver. A time where they *lost money* on a faulty product or bogus service.

Fear of being burned or taken advantage of prevents many people from spending their money. Customers can also be very wary of buying a product or service for the first time. How often do you use the social reviews of your peer group or the comments left on websites to support your buying decisions? We do this to offset our risk. This is why negative reviews are so much more powerful than positive ones, because we move away from pain, we don't move towards pleasure. Change the risk equation so that it favors you.

Providing a strong guarantee eliminates the majority of risk involved in the purchase and breaks down natural barriers in the sales process. Guarantees will often shorten the sales process all together – skipping any discussion of objections – because the customer does not see any risk in "trying the product out."

There is also a growing consumer expectation when it comes to guarantees. Many stores will take back anything the customer has not been happy with and return money or store credit. Popular health food stores encourage customers to try new or unfamiliar products by promising a hassle-free, no questions asked return process. A guarantee or easy return policy can be the difference between choosing one business over its competition.

Your customers buy results, not products or services

The strongest guarantee you can make is on *results*, not products or services.

If you guarantee that your customer will receive the benefits or results for which they are looking, the specific product or service they'll need to achieve those results becomes irrelevant. You have shifted the conversation from a price driven conversation to a value driven conversation.

People buy benefits and results. For example, they don't buy water purifiers; they buy the benefit enjoying clean, fresh-tasting water. They don't buy lawn sprinkler systems; they buy a healthy green lawn.

Once you understand what specific benefit or solution your customers are seeking, find a way to guarantee they'll receive or experience that solution. If they don't, you'll compensate them for it.

Remember what you have guaranteed

While guarantees will increase sales for most businesses, they can also be the fast track to business failure if their product or service isn't a quality one. Take the time to ensure you have a strong offering before you implement a guarantee.

Guarantees are most effective when you are selling someone something they need or want – not when you are trying to convince someone to purchase something they have no use for.

Increasing Conversion Rates with a Guarantee

Guarantees can help your business turn more qualified leads into repeat customers. Strong guarantees are big and bold, but also realistic. They're just a little bit better than your competition, but consistent with the industry's standards.

Your conversion rate

Your conversion rate is the percentage of clients you convert from leads into customers. The higher your conversion rate, the more revenue you will generate.

To figure out your conversion rate, divide the number of people who purchase from you by the number of people who inquired about your product or service. This will generate a percentage value of your conversion rate.

Guarantees encourage and increase conversion. They motivate potential customers to buy – and to buy from you – because you stand behind what you sell in a big way. There is no risk involved in purchasing what you have to offer.

Creating your guarantee

So, you're convinced your business – and your customers – would benefit from a strong guarantee. Now what? What are you going to guarantee? How are you going to position it?

Once again, this goes back to your target audience and your product or service. What are some of the major objections your potential customers raise during the sales process? What kind of risk do they take on when they make a purchase? How much time will they need to test or experience your product or service?

Brainstorm a list of things about your industry that really frustrate your customers. They could be service-based (contractors that don't show up, employees who don't perform) or product-based (products that break, do not perform). Then, take a look at your list and decide how you can make sure these things do not happen. Think big – you can do a lot more than you think – then determine if you can actually make good on your promise. If you can't guarantee the first frustration, then move on to the second.

Here are some tips on writing your guarantee:

- **Be specific**. Explain exactly what you are guaranteeing. Don't make vague guarantees that a product will "work" or a service will make you "happy". These words mean different things to different people. Guarantee specific performance or results.

- **Include a clear timeframe.** Put a realistic timeframe on your guarantee. Very few products or services are good forever. Offer a 30-day or 90-day free trial; guarantee results within a set number of days or weeks. This can protect your company, and sets out clear expectations for your clients.
- **Be bold**. Unbelievable guarantees get a customer's attention, so go as far as you realistically can with your claim. Find a way to stand out over the competition – which may also have a guarantee.
- **Tell them what you'll do**. Explain what you'll do – how you'll compensate them – if your product or service doesn't deliver. Be specific, talk money, and go above and beyond.

Implementing guarantees

Tell your clients!

Put your guarantee everywhere – your website, brochures, receipt tape, in-store signage, advertisements, and other promotional materials. It will only help attract customers if they know about it.

Send a newsletter to your existing client base informing them of your new guarantees – you never know how many customers you can convince to come back and spend more in your business.

Train your Staff

Once you have decided to offer your clients a guarantee, you need to ensure your staff are properly trained on the specific policies and procedures associated with that guarantee. If you offer different guarantees for different products and services, ensure this is made clear as well.

Presumably, your staff will be communicating the details of your guarantee and fielding customer questions. They will have to know how to sell the product using the guarantee as a benefit, understand every application of the guarantee in your business, and relate to every scenario a customer may encounter to use it.

To ensure your staff is not making any false claims or promises, create a guarantee script for them to use and stick to. This will prevent customers from returning with false hopes for their money back, or other compensation.

Returns + Claims

So, by now you must be thinking, "Great, I can convert more customers with a strong guarantee, and increase my sales. But what about the added risk I have taken on from my customers? Won't I start to see a ton of returns and service claims?" This is a valid question. Making a strong guarantee means standing by it and delivering on your promise. Inevitably, when you guarantee something, someone is going to take you up on that guarantee and make a claim. I'm going to answer this question in two parts:

1. Stand behind your product or service. You're not in business to scam customers. If you sell a product or service, and you believe in it enough to offer it to your customers, it is likely a quality product or genuine service.

If this is a concern to you, consider implementing strong quality controls or stronger criteria for your merchandising. Companies that offer products and services that deliver results can offer the strongest guarantees.

Of course, you will get returns. You will have customers come in to take advantage of you. Just remember that as long as the increase in sales outweighs the claims, your guarantee strategy has been successful.

2. Understand your customer's likely behavior. The truth is that most customers will never take advantage of your guarantee – regardless of their satisfaction level. There are a number of reasons for this.

The first is that most people can't be bothered to drive, mail, or otherwise seek a refund on an item under $50. Many let the timeframe slip by and have an "oh well" attitude.

The second is that most people don't like confrontation. There is usually an element of confrontation involved in telling someone you didn't like a product or service, and many people do not have the confidence to do so. They'd rather eat the cost than go through the process of asking for a refund.

Handling claims and returns:

If you do have your product returned, it is in your company's best interest to create a system for handling these customer interactions.

Create a claim form

Ensure that each customer who makes a claim about your product or service fills out a standard form. Doing so will help you prevent fraud, gather important information about the customer and their reasoning, and create a "hoop" for the customer to jump through if they want their money back.

Name
Date
Contact Information
Salesperson
Product
Reason for claim:
Comments
Follow-up

Keep a claim or return log

Create a log or filing system for your claims. This will give you a snapshot of your guarantee program, a record-keeping system, and a wealth of information about each customer's experience and motivations.

Use the information

Take the claim forms your customers have filled out, and review them regularly. While some of the claims won't be genuine, there will be some real feedback you can use to improve your product or service, or to modify your guarantee. You may need to make it more realistic or change the specifics.

7

Create Profitable Sales Letters

In the modern world of billion-dollar ad campaigns, glossy brochures, and sophisticated email marketing, the simple effect of a well-written sales letter is often underestimated, or even forgotten entirely.

Sales letters are a simple and powerful marketing tool that – when written effectively – can generate serious results for your business. In a mailbox full of impersonal brochures that are often perceived to be "junk", a personally addressed letter will be kept and opened for a further look.

The power of sales letters truly lies in the personal nature of the communication. As opposed to brochures and advertising, the sales letter will arrive personally addressed and hand stamped. An effective sales letter will engage the recipient with the first sentence and persuade them to act by speaking to their personal needs and purchase motivations.

You don't need to be an award-winning copywriter to craft a successful sales letter. Some of the best sales letters ever written are not renowned for their grammar or clever word choice – they're known for their customer engagement strategy. The way they told a story that related to the audience and got them to get their wallets.

So then, the true key to writing a successful sales letter is knowing who you're targeting, what their needs are, and how to reach them directly.

Writing an Effective Sales Letter

Step One: Decide Who Your Audience Is

To truly leverage the impact of a personal sales letter, your target audience must be carefully defined. Are you targeting stay-at-home mothers? Do-it-yourself fathers? A particular income bracket, age, or neighborhood? Demographic-specific direct-mail mailing lists are commonly available, and a great tool to access a very targeted group of potential customers.

If you are targeting your existing client base, you may wish to segment your list by recent purchase behavior. For example, categorize customers by the last time they purchased, and send a "miss you!" letter to those who haven't been in to your store in over six months (or another reasonable timeframe).

Keep your target market research close at hand. If you have a highly segmented target market, you may wish to craft a sales letter for each of your segments and mailing lists. Revisit each segment purchase motivations, demographic characteristics, and behavioral characteristics. What do they need? What do they want? What are their common frustrations or hot buttons? What kind of story would they resonate with?

From this information, you will understand how to communicate your offer so that it elicits an emotional response from your readers. An emotional response will motivate them to order, purchase, or support your offering.

Step Two: Choose Your Message (including your offer)

What are you going to tell your readers? Do you have a time-sensitive offer? A solution to their problems or needs? How about a guarantee or a promise? Do you have proof?

You've already established a clear marketing message and USP and have likely created several advertisements and brochures to communicate that message to a broad audience. When writing your sales letter, you need to customize or reframe that message to your specific audience in a way that speaks to their emotions, and clearly describes "what's in it for me?"

Step Three: Write it Down!

Here is a guideline for basic sales letter structure. More templates are included at the end of this chapter.

Headline

Headlines are optional for sales letters but can be an effective way to summarize or communicate your message. Rhetorical questions that speak to a problem or frustration are especially effective. Centre your headline in bold above the greeting line.

Sub Headline + Lead Paragraph

The sub headline and lead paragraph are how you are going to get the reader to care enough to read the rest of the letter. Provide a solution to the problem you raised in your headline or answer the question you posed. Then, in the lead paragraph, briefly describe your offer and the corresponding benefits.

Illustration / Proof

Just like any compelling statement or opinion, you need to back up your claim, guarantee, or offer with an illustration of how it works. If your offer is particularly outrageous, customers are naturally going to respond with a "prove it" attitude.

This is a good opportunity to tell a story or include a testimonial. You can briefly describe the experience of a customer who purchased the offer and follow the story with their real testimonial – emphasized by italics or bold font.

Benefits

Including a summary of product or service benefits in your letter tells the customer that you're thinking about their needs and writing the letter with them in mind. Use "you" and "your" heavily in the text and describe product or service features sparingly.

An effective way to summarize benefits is with a bulleted list near the end of the letter, with key phrases in bold type.

Close / Call to Action

Give them a reason to pick up the phone, fill out the order form, or return the stamped envelope *immediately*. Without an incentive to act, your readers will put your letter in their to-do list and may never "get around" to closing the deal.

Incentives can include time-based or supply-based urgency – "Offer valid this month only," or "Only 50 available" – or the inclusion of a bonus item when the sale is completed by a stated date.

Tips for Putting it All Together

Keep it professional. Put the letter on your business letterhead, and send it in a hand-stamped, high-quality envelope. Letters sent on non-descript envelopes with metered postage are impersonal and look like mass junk-mail.

Make it easy to take action. Include prepaid envelopes, easy to fill out order forms, toll-free phone numbers, email links, and website addresses. The easier it is for the customer to act, the more likely they will. Provide several options for action, if possible, so the customer can choose an option that is most convenient for them.

Professional, but not formal. Write as though you're speaking with a family member or friend. Casual, colloquial language will help to build trust with your reader, as it establishes that you are on the "same level" and can relate to the same needs and problems.

Tell a story. Engage the reader with a story that relates to your offer or ask. If you have a compelling customer testimonial, consider beginning your letter with that. People are interested in the stories and experiences of others, so this is a highly persuasive writing strategy.

Make an announcement or tell a secret. Start your letter off with a shocking announcement that includes or relates to your offer. This can be new research statistics, a new development or invention, or a celebrity testimonial. News that is just barely believable will engage the reader to read more…

Identify a problem, then solve it. Use the headline to ask a question that identifies a common problem, then show how your offer can solve it. For example, "Hate drying the dishes *after* they've been through the dishwasher?" or "How many more times will you have to ask your kids to make their beds this year?" This puts you on common ground with your reader and makes them assume the body of the letter has the solution!

Establish credibility. This needs to be done as soon as possible in your letter. If your readers do not believe in your credibility by the second or third paragraph, the chances of closing the sale have greatly diminished. Explain who the company is, and why you're worth the reader's attention. Use accolades, awards, and testimonials to prove your point – the words of others will be trusted over your own.

Make it useful or memorable. Just like a business card, you can encourage your reader to keep the letter if it provides something of use. If you are a dentist, include the top 10 best snack foods for kids. Include a fridge magnet with your contact information, or perhaps another small gift that is branded with your company logo and website address.

Build relationships. Establish trust. Use the sales letter to establish a long-term relationship with each recipient on your target market list. Seek to establish their needs and wants and show how you can meet them. Avoid pushy language and pressure tactics that get you the sale, but not the customer.

Make mistakes. When you're sending out your first few mailings and learning about your target audience, consider sending a few different letters to your list to see what works best. Testing your audience will help you learn their hot buttons and purchase motivations, and ultimately refine your ability to communicate with them in a way that generates sales dollars.

Use the postscript. After your closing and signature, consider re-stating your offer in the postscript (PS). It is one more opportunity to remind customers of a limited-time or limited-quantity offer to act quickly.

Include a brochure. A short brochure or factsheet can add graphic proof to back up your claims. This can include product imagery, research charts and graphs, or images of customers with accompanying testimonials.

Pay attention to formatting. Accept the fact that most readers will skim your letter until they find a reason to pay more thorough attention. This can work for you, if you format your letter to accommodate it. When you're finished, test the formatting by reading only headlines, sub headlines and bold text. Do all your messages come across clearly?

- Give important paragraphs a sub headline
- Make sure paragraphs are different lengths
- Use colors and boldface type to highlight key words or messages

Types of Sales Letters

Potential Client

A letter to a new client is intended to introduce your business and interest your reader in what you have to say and offer. The incentive to act is less aggressive than other letters, and the focus of the letter is on how the benefits of your product or service will solve the reader's problems and meet their needs.

Unique Selling Proposition

This type of sales letter puts a heavy focus on how your product or service soars about the competition and gives your reader a strong incentive to act quickly. These tend to be more aggressive letters that work well with existing clients, or clients you have begun to build a relationship with.

Referral

A referral letter is used when an associate has referred a potential client to you. It is important to include in the first paragraph the name of the contact that referred you, and why they felt the potential client could use your products or services.

Relationship Building

Use a relationship building letter to follow up with customers who have already purchased from you. This will let them know that you care about their experience with your product, and that you are available if they need assistance. This type of letter will also allow you keep your customer informed of changes and developments within your business and its employees. The benefit of sending regular follow up letters is that your business is kept top of mind for the next purchase, or when existing clients are asked for referrals by their family and friends.

Job Transition

A job transition letter is an important tool when you are changing organizations or taking over territory from another representative. The intent is either to encourage your customers to follow you to your new organization, or to reassure customers that you will continue to provide high quality service in place of your colleague. Make sure to include all your pertinent contact information, and perhaps offer to meet with customers to introduce yourself personally.

Meeting Request

If you phone calls requesting a meeting have been buried under a list of voicemails, a short letter requesting a meeting or presentation time may have more impact. Keep this type of letter short and friendly and remind the reader of what your product or service can do for them.

Closing

Use a closing letter to "seal the deal" and encourage the customer to commit. This type of letter is typically used as follow up to a meeting or presentation, and requests another meeting to finalize arrangements. Again, remind the reader what your product or service can do for them, and offer to provide more information if it is required.

Templates

Potential Client

[Headline in bold at the top of the page – strong statement or question]

[Optional sub headline to explain or answer the question/statement]

Dear [name],

Opening this letter may be the best thing you've done today. [Company name] is your answer to [list common problem or need here].

Over the past [number] years, we have built our business on [insert customer-focused value or belief]. We strive to ensure every customer is satisfied with their purchase, and [insert guarantee, if applicable].

Take a look at the enclosed [brochure/catalogue/marketing piece]. When you purchase [product/service], don't be surprised if you experience:

- *[list benefits in bullet form]*
- *[list benefits in bullet form]*
- *[list benefits in bullet form]*

To thank you for your time, when you [call / purchase / register], mention this letter and receive [insert discount / free gift / free service]. We look forward to working with you.

Sincerely,
[your name]

Unique Selling Proposition

[Headline in bold at the top of the page – strong statement or question]

[Optional sub headline to explain or answer the question/statement]

Dear [name],

Did *you know [insert shocking statement of fact with a number or statistic attached – ensure this relates to the problem you will solve or need you will meet]? We didn't either.*

[Use the second paragraph to elaborate on the statement and connect the problem to the its solution: your product or service]. In addition to [solved problem here], our [product/service] will:

[list benefits in bullet form]

Our [product/service name] is guaranteed to [insert benefit or solution here] because [describe how this product/service is unique from or better than the competition].

Just let those who have already purchased [product/service] speak for themselves:

[include testimonials here]

Sincerely,
[your name]
[company name]
[phone number]

PS – Remember, with just a quick phone call today and not only will your [quickly state problem that will be solved], but you will [save money, receive a free gift, etc.]

Referral

Dear [name],

I received your contact information from [insert referee name here], who suggested I contact you regarding your [insert problem, need or want here].

I am the [insert title/position] with [insert company name], and we specialize in [insert product or service type] for [insert type of customer]. Our [product/service] has [include prime example or illustration of the benefits of your product/service] for over [insert age] years.

Since [insert referee name] became a customer in [insert year or month], we have been [describe how the benefits of your product/service have been helping others].

Enclosed you will find a [brochure, catalogue, or other marketing piece] for further information on the [product/service] we offer.

I would love the opportunity to meet with you to further discuss how our [insert product or service] can assist you with [insert problem/need/issue]. I will be in touch with you directly next week to arrange a meeting time.

Sincerely,
[your name]
[company name]

Relationship Building

Dear [name],

Thank you for choosing [company name] for your [product/service] purchase earlier this month [week/year]. We hope the [product/service] is [serving your needs / solving your problem] as you envisioned.

I would like to remind you that we offer [insert complementary products, product maintenance services, and other ways you can continue to serve the customer's needs.]

I would also like to let you know that [insert company news, staff promotions, product or service expansions, etc.]. We are growing our business to support the needs of customers like you.

Please feel free to contact me if you ever need anything else, [insert phone number here].

Sincerely,
[your name]
[company name]
[phone number]

Job Transition

Dear [name],

I hope you are enjoying the [weather/season change/other recent event to set up friendly nature of the letter].

In the spirit of change, I am writing to let know that I have accepted a new role with [insert company name], a provider of [product/service description].

[Company name] is known for [insert product/service point of difference] and prides itself on [insert value and benefit of product/service]. I believe you would benefit from [list or describe benefit of new product/service].

I have always enjoyed working with you, since you became a customer of [past company name] in [year/month]. As an existing client of mine, I would like to offer you [describe exclusive offer, discount, free gift].

Please note my new contact information below. I will call you to this week to chat about how I can continue to be of service to you with [company name].

Warm regards,
[your name]
[company name]
[phone number]

Meeting Request

Dear [name],

I have tried to reach you on the phone this week but have not been able to connect with you directly. I was calling to introduce myself and my company, [insert company name], which [insert brief description of what your company can offer here].

I understand that you / your company [insert what recipient company does] and may [insert needs, wants, or other requirements].

Our company was established in [insert year here] to [insert company purpose/vision – a solution to a potential problem/need the recipient has].

We have recently [expanded/decided to reach out to our community – insert reason for contacting recipient now] and would like to meet with you to discuss how [insert product or service] can [insert need/problem here].

I will follow up with you on the phone later this week. Alternately, please feel free to contact me at your convenience at [insert phone number here].

Sincerely,
[your name]
[company name]
[phone number]

Closing

Dear [name],

Thank you for meeting with me on [date]. I trust you and your partners have had time to consider our presentation and discuss our offer to [describe offer to provide product or service here].

At [company name], we pride ourselves on high quality [products/services] and customer satisfaction. [Briefly restate USP and product/service benefits].

We have a solid understanding of [describe requirements/needs] and believe our company can [describe solutions]. Remember that we offer a [state company guarantee}.

I would like to stop by on [date + time] to finalize our agreement so we can start working together right away. Please confirm if this is a good time for you.

Sincerely,
[your name]
[company name]
[phone number]

Top 5 Sales Letters of All Time

Below you will find five of the best sales letters of all time – written for some of the most well-known businesses and publications of our time. Take time to review them carefully and establish what makes them so engaging and convincing.

American Express: The "Quite Frankly" Letter

This letter immediately hooks the reader with an "are you good enough?" statement. The reader will continue reading to prove that he is, indeed, good enough for Amex.

Dear Mr. Smith:

Quite frankly, the American Express Card is not for everyone. And not everyone who applies for Card membership is approved.

However, because we believe you will benefit from Card Membership, I've enclosed a special invitation for you to apply for the most honored and prestigious financial instrument available to people who travel, vacation, and entertain.

The American Express Card is the perfect example of the old adage, "You get what you pay for." For example, you get a truly impressive array of extra privileges, all designed for your convenience and security:

A Worldwide Network of Travel Service Offices* is at your Service. Enjoy personal attention at any of the nearby 1,000 American Express Offices -- Your "homes away from home" --around the globe.

Cash your Personal Check at Thousands of Locations. Cash up to $250 at participating hotels and motels, and up to $1,000 at most American Express Travel Services Offices all over the world. (Subject to cash availability and local regulations.)

Card Lost or Stolen? You'll Get a Quick Replacement. If the Card is lost or stolen, an emergency replacement will be provided at any Travel Service Office in the world, usually by the end of the next business day.

Obtain Emergency Funds Instantly. Once you've enrolled in this convenient service, our network of automated Travelers Check Dispensers lets you obtain up to $500 ... in 60 seconds or less!

Carry $100,000 of Travel Accident Insurance. Just charge your tickets to the Card, and you, your spouse or dependent children under the age of 23 are automatically covered when traveling by common carrier on land, sea, or in the air. It's underwritten by Fireman's Fund Insurance Companies, San

Rafael, California, for approximately 35 cents of the annual Card Membership fee.

Your Hotel Reservations are Assured. As an American Express Card Member, if you request, your hotel room will be held for you until checkout the following day at nearly 8,000 participating hotels.

Enjoy Special Express Hotel Service. Speedy check-in and checkout is available to Card Members at more than 1,000 hotels, including Hilton, Hyatt, Marriott, Sheraton, and more.

Extras like these only begin to tell the story of American Express Card security, emergency protection, and convenience. You'll also enjoy:

Unequalled Mobility. The Card is welcomed by the world's major airlines, car rental agencies, railroads, and cruise lines. Plus, it pays for auto parts and servicing at thousands of locations nationwide.

A Worldwide Welcome. Fine restaurants, hotel resorts, and a host of other establishments around this world, and right in your hometown, recognize the Card and welcome your patronage.

Purchasing Power. No need to carry large amounts of cash. The Card takes care of shopping needs, whether you're choosing a wardrobe, buying theater tickets, sending flowers, or hosting a dinner (even if you can't be there!)

Financial Freedom. Unlike bank cards, the American Express Card imposes no pre-set spending limit. Purchases are approved based on your ability to pay as demonstrated by your past spending, payment patterns, and personal *resources. So you are free to make your own decisions about when and where to use the Card.*

In a few words, American Express Card Membership is the most effective letter of introduction to the world of travel, entertainment, and the good life yet devised. Yet surprisingly, these benefits are all yours to enjoy for the modest fee of just $35 a year.

Why not apply for Card Membership today? All you have to do is fill out and mail the enclosed application. As soon as it is approved, we'll send along the Card, without delay.

Sincerely,
Diane Shalb
Vice President
P.S. Apply today and enjoy all the benefits of Card Membership. Those listed here are just a handful of what's available. A full listing is included in the Guide to Card Member Services you'll receive along with the Card.

Newsweek: the letter that built a media powerhouse

Dear Reader:

If the list upon which I found your name is any indication, this is not the first -- nor will it be the last -- subscription letter you receive. Quite frankly, your education and income set you apart from the general population and makes you a highly-rated prospect for everything from magazines to mutual funds.

You've undoubtedly 'heard everything' by now in the way of promises and premiums. I won't try to top any of them. Nor will I insult your intelligence.

If you subscribe to Newsweek, you won't get rich quick. You won't bowl over friends and business associates with clever remarks and sage comments after your first copy of Newsweek arrives. (Your conversation will benefit from a better understanding of the events and forces of our era, but that's all. Wit and wisdom are gifts no magazine can bestow.) And should you attain further professional or business success during the term of your subscription, you'll have your own native ability and good luck to thank for it -- not Newsweek.

What, then, can Newsweek do for you?

The answer depends upon what type of person you happen to be. If you are not curious about what's going on outside your own immediate daily range of concern...if you are quickly bored when the topic of conversation shifts from your house, your car, your ambitions...if you couldn't care less about what's happening in Washington or Wall Street, in London or Moscow...then forget Newsweek. It can't do a thing for you.

If, on the other hand, you are the kind of individual who would like to keep up with national and international affairs, space and nuclear science, the arts -- but cannot spend hours at it...if you're genuinely interested in what's going on with other members of the human race...if you recognize the big stake you have in decisions made in Washington and Wall Street, in London and Moscow...then Newsweek may well be the smartest investment you could make in the vital weeks and months ahead!

For little more than 1¢ a day, as a Newsweek subscriber, your interest in national and international affairs will be served by over 200 top-notch reporters here and around the world. Each week, you'll read the most significant facts taken from their daily dispatches by Newsweek's editors.

You'll get the facts. No bias. No slanting. Newsweek respects your right to form your own opinion.

In the eventful weeks to come, you'll read about:

- Election strategy (Who will run against JFK? Medicare, education, unemployment: how will they sway voters?)

- Administration moves (New civil-rights bill in the works? Taxes: what next?)

- G.O.P. plans (Stepped-up activity in Dixie? New faces for Congressional races?)

- Kremlin maneuverings (Will Cold War policies change? New clashes with Red China?)

- Europe's future (New leaders, new programs? How can America compete with the Common Market?)

You'll also keep on top of latest developments in the exciting fields of space and nuclear science. Whether the story describes a space-dog's trip to Venus or the opening of a new area in the peaceful use of atomic fission, you'll learn the key facts in Newsweek's Space & The Atom feature -- the first and only weekly department devoted to space and nuclear science in any newsweekly.

The fascinating world of art will be reviewed and interviewed for you in Newsweek. Whether you are interested in books or ballet, painting or plays, movies or music -- or all of them -- you will find it covered fully and fairly in Newsweek.

Subscribe now and you'll read about international film awards...new art shows at the Louvre in Paris...the opening of the Metropolitan and La Scala opera seasons...glittering first nights on and off Broadway...plus revealing interviews with famed authors and prima donnas, actors and symphony conductors.

AND you'll be briefed on happenings in the worlds of Business and Labor (More wage demands now?) ...Education and Religion (Reforms in teacher training? More church mergers?) ...Science and Medicine (Cancer, arthritis cures on the way?)...Sports and TV-Radio (New world records? More educational TV, fewer MD shows?)

You read Newsweek at your own pace. Its handy Top of the Week index lets you scan the top news stories of the week in two minutes. When you have a lull in your busy schedule, you can return to the story itself for full details. In this way, you are assured of an understanding of the events and forces of our era.

TRY Newsweek.

Try it at our special introductory offer:

37 WEEKS OF NEWSWEEK FOR ONLY $2.97

That's about 8 ¢ a week -- little more than a penny a day. You would pay $9.25 at newsstands for the same number of copies; $4.98 at our regular yearly subscription rates.

And try it with this guarantee: if, after examining several issues in your own home, you do not agree that Newsweek satisfies your news interests, you will receive a prompt refund.

An order form is enclosed, along with a postage-paid return envelope. Do initial and return the order form today. We'll bill you later, if you wish.

Sincerely,

S. Arthur Dembner
Circulation Director

Wall Street Journal: Martin Conroy's "Two Young Men" Letter

This letter has run for 28 years in a row, and continues to pull in new subscribers for WSJ.

Dear Reader:

On a beautiful late spring afternoon, twenty-five years ago, two young men graduated from the same college. They were very much alike, these two young men. Both had been better than average students, both were personable and both -- as young college graduates are -- were filled with ambitious dreams for the future.

Recently, these men returned to their college for their 25th reunion. They were still very much alike. Both were happily married. Both had three children. And both, it turned out, had gone to work for the same Midwestern manufacturing company after graduation, and were still there.

But there was a difference. One of the men was manager of a small department of that company. The other was its president.

What Made The Difference

Have you ever wondered, as I have, what makes this kind of difference in people's lives? It isn't always a native intelligence or talent or dedication. It isn't that one person wants success and the other doesn't.

The difference lies in what each person knows and how he or she makes use of that knowledge. And that is why I am writing to you and to people like you about The Wall Street Journal. For that is the whole purpose of The Journal: To give its readers knowledge - knowledge that they can use in business.

A Publication Unlike Any Other

You see, The Wall Street Journal is a unique publication. It's the country's only national business daily. Each business day, it is put together by the world's largest staff for business-news experts.

Each business day, The Journal's pages include a broad range of information of interest and significance to business-minded people, no matter where it comes from. Not just stocks and finance, but anything and everything in the whole, fast-moving world of business ... The Wall Street Journal gives you all the business news you need — when you need it.

Knowledge Is Power

Right now, I am reading page one of The Journal. It combines all the important news of the day with in-depth feature reporting. Every phase of business news is covered, from articles on inflation, wholesale prices, car prices, tax incentives for industries to major developments in Washington, and elsewhere.

And there is page after page inside The Journal filled with fascinating and significant information that's useful to you. A daily column on personal money management helps you become a smarter saver, better investor, wiser spender. There are weekly columns on small business, marketing, real estate, technology, regional developments. If you have never read The Wall Street Journal, you cannot imagine how useful it can be to you.

Much of the information that appears in The Journal appears nowhere else. The Journal is printed in numerous plants across the United States, so that you get it early each business day.

A $28 Subscription

Put our statements to the proof by subscribing for the next 13 weeks for just $28. This is the shortest subscription term we offer - and a perfect way to get acquainted with The Journal.

Or you may prefer to take advantage of a longer-term subscription for greater savings: an annual subscription at $107 saves you $20 off The Journal's cover price. Our best buy — two years for $185 - saves you a full $69!

Simply fill out the endorsed order card and mail it in the postage-paid envelope provided. And here's The Journal guarantee: Should The Journal not measure up to your expectations, you may cancel this trial arrangement at any point and receive a refund for the undelivered portion of your subscription.

If you feel as we do that this is a fair and reasonable proposition, then you will want to find out without delay if The Wall Street Journal can do for you what it is doing for millions of readers. So please mail the enclosed order card now, and we will start serving you immediately.

About those two college classmates, I mention at the beginning of this letter. They graduated from college together and together got started in the business world. So what made their lives in business different?

Knowledge. Useful knowledge. And its application.

An Investment In Success

I cannot promise you that success will be instantly yours if you start reading The Wall Street Journal. But I can guarantee that you will find The Journal always interesting, always reliable, and always useful.

Sincerely Yours,
Peter R. Kann
Executive Vice President/
Associate Publisher

P.S. It's important to note that The Journal's subscription price may be tax-deductible.

Xerox: Preferred Account Status Letter

Dear Mr. Smith:

We believe you should get credit for buying office products directly from Xerox.

That's why I'd like you to be among the first to enjoy the many privileges of the new Xerox Preferred Account -- absolutely free. All you have to do is sign and return the enclosed authorization form. Your Preferred Account status will bring these exclusive and outstanding benefits:

1. The opportunity to buy office products directly from Xerox -- at incredibly low prices;

2. Special Preferred Account bonus offers on a wide range of Xerox products;

3. The ability to charge not only purchases but equipment service directly to your Preferred Account;

4. The convenience of ordering products by phone (toll-free) through your own, personal Preferred Account Telephone Representative;

5. All purchases are backed by Xerox's reputation for quality and dependability. If for any reason you are not completely satisfied, return your purchase within 15 days and pay nothing;

6. Preferred Account holders receive first notice on all new Xerox products and services.

Best of all, your Xerox Preferred Account qualifies you for an initial $3,000 line of instant credit which you can use at any time.

There's no minimum purchase requirement. No fee or service charge. No risk or obligation whatsoever.

That alone makes the Xerox Preferred Account one of the most flexible credit lines you hold. You'll receive one convenient, completely-itemized statement each month.

In summary, the Xerox Preferred Account offers you everything you need to equip your office -- from typewriters to copiers, professional computers to printers. And the convenience of financing, too!

Your pre-approved Acceptance Form is enclosed. Simply complete it, sign it and mail it back to us. Postage has already been paid for you.

Or call our Preferred Account Center at 1-800-828-9090 (toll-free) if you have any questions or require assistance.

Please let me hear from you before August 15th. That way you'll be able to take advantage of all the product and service discounts we'll be offering in the near future.

Remember, there's no fee, obligation or risk involved in opening a Xerox Preferred Account. It's simply our way of making it easy for you to get the best office products and service available -- at special direct prices.

Remember too, your instant line of credit has already been approved. So, sign and mail your Acceptance Form today.

On behalf of everyone at Team Xerox, I am pleased to offer you this invitation to open a Preferred Account with us. I look forward to your acceptance.

Sincerely,
Scott Seeman Manager
Preferred Accounts
P.S. As a Bonus Enrollment Offer, we are extending you a special discount on our 605 and 610 Memory writers through August 15th. Please see the enclosed

Product Information sheet. This is just one example of the many values you'll enjoy with a Xerox Preferred Account.

Popular Mechanics: Average Joe Letter

Good Friend,

This invitation isn't for deadbeats, rip-off artists or "gentlemen" who hate to get their hands dirty. It's for the rest of us. It's for the average guy who works hard for a living (and wants to live better). Who knows the value of a buck (about 50 ¢ these days). Who is willing to trade a few drops of sweat for the chance to save big bucks.

It's for guys who aren't afraid to get down under the sink with a pipe wrench. Guys who don't mind sticking their hands in the toilet tank to adjust a ball cock (because they know it's going to save a $16 plumber's bill).

Our country was built on the sweat and hard work of do-it-yourself guys. And from POPULAR MECHANICS, the #1 do-it-yourself magazine, we'd just like to say THANK YOU.

Our big, illustrated POPULAR MECHANICS DO-IT-YOURSELF ENCYCLOPEDIA was written with "shirtsleeves" guys in mind. Guys like you. So please -- let me ship you Volume I FREE. (No strings attached. No purchase necessary.)

It's BIG -- 168 oversized pages crammed with up-to-date money-saving plans, photos, diagrams and articles about how-to-do just about EVERYTHING!

From fixing your car's alternator to improving your gas mileage by 30 percent!

From drilling an angled hole accurately, to resurfacing your asphalt driveway or fixing a small appliance.

It's PRACTICAL -- oversized pages lay down flat so you have them right there on your shop table or car fender to refer to. Sturdy hard-covers laugh at dirt! Type is LARGE so it's easy-to-read.

Each article is generously illustrated -- Volume I alone has more than 600 step-by-step drawings, photos and diagrams.

SPEAKING OF SAVING, HAVE YOU BEEN TO A BODY SHOP LATELY? If it was within the past 12 months you know the cost of auto body repairs has zoomed out of sight!

So, we got the manager of a big body shop near our office to share his trade secrets with us. The results? An article illustrated with how-to-do-it photos that shows you how to get rid of scratches, dents, rust and rotten spots yourself -- make your fender look like new!

All this, and much more, is in Volume I of the POPULAR MECHANICS D0-IT-YOURSELF ENCYCLOPEDIA.

But remember -- you don't pay a cent for it. Now or ever. And there's no obligation -- NO PURCHASE NECESSARY!

"Well, come on," you're probably saying, "There's gotta be a catch." MAYBE THERE IS. Sure, I'd like to sell you the whole POPULAR MECHANICS DO-IT-YOURSELF ENCYCLOPEDIA.

But I know from experience that I can't "sell" someone like you. You've got to prove for yourself it's worthwhile. So, accept our FREE book and examine Volume I, then make up your own mind.

VOLUME I IS YOUR FREE SAMPLE. AND I WANT YOU TO USE IT FOR ALL IT'S WORTH.

Got kids? Turn to page 50 for complete plans and instructions for making your own hockey tabletop game. (You'll have a ball with it, too.) It would cost you plenty in a store. But you can make it with a few dollars' worth of lumber, particleboard, and an old range exhaust fan.

Want a greenhouse? On pages 30-32 you'll find plans for an elegant addition -- an add -on Greenhouse.

How about valuable antiques? Why not build your own authentic reproduction pine and maple bench...for a fraction of what an original would cost. Complete plans and instructions start on Page 30.

Turn to page 178 to see how easy it is to do all your own routine auto service and maintenance. (If you're spending $200 a year to have a pro do it, you could save $150!)

Cool your house in the summer (and cut your air conditioning electric bills) by installing an attic fan. The article starting on page 156 shows you how.

I could go on and on. But why should I? Volume I of POPULAR MECHANICS DO-IT-YOURSELF ENCYCLOPEDIA is yours for the asking.

You don't even pay to send for it. Postage paid Reply Card enclosed. So, what are you waiting for? Say YES today!

When your "Free Sample" arrives, keep it. And use it. And see for yourself why POPULAR MECHANICS is usually considered the world's leading source of "do-it-yourself" information.

NOW LISTEN TO THIS.

If Volume I isn't everything I've promised, just drop us a note saying "No more!" That will be the end of it (of course, you keep Volume I). But if you're as pleased as I expect, just sit back and enjoy your Free Volume. Then, eight weeks later, you'll receive Volume II of the POPULAR MECHANICS DO-IT-YOURSELF ENCYCLOPEDIA --just as big, beautiful, husky and crammed with plans and information as the first one. For example:

HOW TO TEST & RECHARGE MOST BATTERIES...BUILD YOUR OWN BARBECUE BAR... FINISH YOUR BASEMENT LIKE A PRO... PUT IN A STAIRWELL...INSTALL A HALF-BATH ANYWHERE.PLUS EVERYTHING YOU OUGHT TO KNOW ABOUT BANDSAWS...HOW TO

REMOVE A BEARING WALL...ALL ABOUT BELT SANDERS...CHOOSING THE RIGHT BIKE...AND MUCH, MUCH MORE!

That's just a sample of Volume II. But remember -- YOU HAVEN'T YET SPENT OR RISKED A PENNY!

Because Volume II is yours to examine and use freely for 14 days! Then, if you're not completely "sold" on the POPULAR MECHANICS DO-IT-YOURSELF ENCYCLOPEDIA, just return it before the Free Examination Period is over and owe nothing.

By now, however, if you're the kind of guy I think you are, you should be itching to get your hands on the remaining 18 volumes of the POPULAR MECHANICS DO-IT-YOURSELF ENCYCLOPEDIA. If so, when Volume II arrives, simply remit the low subscriber price of only $5.95 plus a small charge for shipping & handling and any applicable sales tax.

Then, the remaining volumes will be sent to you over a five-month period -- each shipment strictly "on approval." Pay for each volume (one payment a month) at the low subscriber price of only $5.95 -- or return it within the 14-day Free-Examination Period and owe nothing.

BUY AS FEW OR AS MANY VOLUMES AS YOU WISH. CANCEL ANY TIME!

Remember -- Volume I of the POPULAR MECHANICS DO-IT-YOURSELF ENCYCLOPEDIA is your "Free Sample" -- yours to keep, even if you decide not to buy anything.

But to get it, you have to sign and mail the enclosed Reply Card.

Do it today.

Cordially,
J. Michael Walters
For POPULAR MECHANICS

P.S. *If you take pride in work well done, want to give your family the better things in life...then you need POPULAR MECHANICS how-to-do-it information on AIR CONDITIONERS...*

BARBECUES...BOATS...BIRDHOUSES...BOOKCASES...BURGLAR ALARMS...CAULKING...CAMERAS...CONCRETE...CLOCKS...DOORS...DRILL PRESSES...ENGINES...FAUCETS...FENCES...GUNS...GETTING IN SHAPE...HEATERS... INSULATION...KITCHENS...KITS...LANDSCAPING...METALWORKING...OUTBOARDS...PAINTING...PLUMBING...PLYWOOD...REMODELING...ROOFS...RAIN GUTTERS...SEPTIC TANKS...SEWING CENTERS...SKIN DIVING...SOLAR ENERGY...SWIMMING POOLS...TILE...TOOLS... TOYS...TRAILERS...TREES...UPHOLSTERY...VACATION HOMES...VACUUMS...WINDOWS... WOODWORKING.

These are just a few of the subjects covered in the 20 volume POPULAR MECHANICS DO-IT-YOURSELF ENCYCLOPEDIA. And Volume I is yours to keep -- but only if you mail the Reply Card NOW!

8

Profit Over the Phone

For some, the word 'telemarketing' brings up images of rows of people with headsets, all working from a head office in a country far, far away.

Others think of the people who always seem to call the minute they take their first bite of dinner. Some just think it's an old-fashioned marketing strategy. While in some cases this may be true, telemarketing is still an important tool for every business – of every size.

What if I were to tell you that you were *already* using telemarketing as a regular part of your business? In fact, telemarketing is re-emerging as a powerful way to generate leads and close sales. Done well, it's also efficient and cost effective.

Every time the people who work your front end pick up the phone, they're engaging in a telemarketing process. Every time one of your salespeople picks up the phone, they too are engaging in a telemarketing process.

Telemarketing is not just a system for cold calls. It's any type of formal communication between your company and its clients over the phone.

So, now you know that you're already doing it, let's talk about how to turn telemarketing into a profitable marketing strategy for your business.

Telemarketing for Your Business

A common misconception is that telemarketing needs to happen on a broad scale in order to be effective. Pages and pages of potential customers must be cold called on a daily basis. Businesses must hire dozens of staff members to conduct and manage the efforts.

Like I mentioned above, telemarketing is any kind of formal communication that happens between a company and a potential or existing client over the phone. Regardless of the size of your business, you can train you existing staff members to effectively use the telephone to generate more leads and convert more sales.

The benefits of establishing an organized telemarketing system are:

- **Instant access.** Reach key decision-makers immediately.
- **One-on-one interaction.** Develop real relationships with empathy and trust.
- **Minimal cost.** Spend less on sales outreach and research.

Who are the Best Telemarketers?

Success in telemarketing has a lot to do with the personality of your company's representative. Generally, good telemarketers have the following qualities and abilities:

- Energy and enthusiasm
- Positive attitude
- Good phone manner
- Empathy
- Belief in your company and its products
- Strong listening skills
- Ability to think on-the-spot
- Ability to handle objection and rejection
- Good organizational skills

The Telemarketing Process

There are two types of telemarketing: outgoing and incoming. You should have a proactive strategy in place to handle both types.

Remember that your approach to telemarketing must have a clear objective; a clear purpose. What is the purpose of the call (outgoing and incoming)? Is it to inform? Set up an appointment? Establish a need or desire? This will help guide how you handle each type.

Incoming Calls

When a customer calls your business for the first time, you should have a system in place to make a great, customer service-oriented impression. Many of these customers will have seen one of your advertisements, received a direct mail piece, or be responding to any other element of your marketing campaign.

Your telemarketing strategy for incoming phone calls can take the form of:

- An answering service
- Voice mail
- A messaging service
- An order taking system
- An information provision system

The person – or people – who answer incoming calls should be well trained for the role and clearly understand the expectations for handling them. Your receptionist should be trained thoroughly in the products and services you sell so he can answer basic customer questions intelligently. Your team should know how to answer the phone according to your company policy, and have excellent phone manners.

Consider including the following instructions into your incoming telemarketing system or process:

- Answer the phone after two and before four rings
- Have a standard company greeting. Include your company name, as well as the name of the person answering the phone.
- Ensure sufficient customer information is recorded. Determine what information is important to gain from each caller.
- Do not place anyone on hold for longer than 20 seconds. Instead, take their name and number and have their call returned promptly.
- Establish a short description of your company's process or point of difference at some point during the phone call.
- Always repeat back any information or agreement exchanged.
- Be the last one to hang up.

Outgoing Calls

Outgoing calls are the more challenging aspect of your telemarketing strategy. In this case you are proactively asking your customer for something, as opposed to responding once they've already been convinced to act.

You can use an outgoing telemarketing strategy to:

- Set appointments
- Generate leads
- Make cold calls
- Update databases
- Follow up on direct mail and other campaigns
- Convert leads to sales
- Conduct surveys

Your outgoing phone call needs to engage the person on the other end and begin to build a relationship based solely on verbal communication (i.e., without the assistance of non-verbal cues and behaviors). Depending on the type of call, you will be seeking to:

- Attract their attention
- Spark their interest, needs, or desires
- Motivate them to act
- Seek agreement

It is essential to the success of your outgoing telemarketing efforts that you create a script for each type of outgoing call your company makes. This will keep you – and your staff – focused on the purpose of the call and give you tools and prompts to keep you on track. We will review scripts for telemarketing later in this chapter.

Here are some simple steps for making your outgoing telemarketing efforts a success:

Know who you are calling

Do your research. Know exactly who it is you need to contact at each company. Is it the manager or vice-president? Owner or CEO? Once you know who you are targeting, you can do some research prior to your phone call, and ensure you call at a time that is convenient. You will want to know a bit about their industry as well as the company and their role within it. If you have served another client in the same industry, let them know.

When you have them on the phone, confirm that the basic information you have is correct (name, title, etc.). If you do not know who the best person to speak to is, ask the receptionist for the name of the person who makes purchasing decisions related to your product.

Be prepared; stay organized

Have all the materials you may need in front of you, and clear your desk of any distractions. Have a notepad handy, and record key elements of the conversation for action or later discussion. Also, keep a record of all the calls you make, and the results of each call. This will prevent you from making duplicate calls, which do not reflect well on your organization, as well as track left messages and the most productive times of the day for outgoing phone calls.

Know why you are calling

Like I mentioned above, your phone calls should be purpose-focused. Are you calling to set up a meeting? Introduce yourself and your products? Get them to try what you have to offer? Keep this clear in your mind and stick to it.

Get past the gatekeeper

To reach busy decision makers, you will have to get past the person who screens unsolicited phone calls: the gatekeeper, assistant, or secretary. Do not assume you will be able to speak to them with the first phone call – it may take two, three, or even seven tries until you are successful. Here are some guidelines for developing a relationship with the gatekeeper:

- Ask for their name and write it down
- Do not underestimate the power of developing a relationship with them
- Get an understanding of their position and responsibilities
- Stay positive and confident
- Never pitch the receptionist on your product
- Once you have developed a relationship, ask them to help you pin the decision-maker down

Be persistent

Persistence pays off – especially when it comes to large potential accounts. You may have to call many times before you can work your way through the gatekeeper, to the person you wish to speak to. Expect this, stay positive, and your persistence will pay off.

Use strong phone skills

You can create a great first impression on the phone when you cultivate great phone communication skills. Pay attention to the tone of your voice, whether or not you are smiling, the pacing of your sentences (slower is better), and general phone manners. Ensure you clearly identify who you are and what company you work for every time you speak to someone new.

Telemarketing Scripts

Scripts are essential to successful telemarketing. You and your employees will benefit having a "plan of action" for every type of phone call that your company makes. This will also ensure that each staff member has a consistent approach, which is part of your branding.

We discussed the importance of scripts and writing scripts earlier in the program, but I encourage you to review the section before you craft your telemarketing scripts.

Here is a list of components you will need to include in your scripts:

Greeting: Opening the Conversation

Your incoming calls should be handled with a consistent, friendly greeting that informs the customer of what company (or department) they've reached and who they're talking to.

Outgoing calls need to engage the customer within the first few moments, just as a headline needs to catch the reader's instant attention. Say just enough to pique their interest and keep them listening, then begin to explain why you are calling.

The opening conversation should be simple and focused on developing a relationship. Ask casual questions and use small talk to put the caller at ease, but don't go on too long. You don't want to appear to be wasting their time.

Reason for your Call

If someone asks why you are calling, tell them. Be up front about why you are calling; clearly state your objectives, then back them up with an explanation that includes benefits to the customer.

You may wish to ask permission before you get into an explanation. Asking, "do you mind if I tell you exactly why I called today?" shows respect for the customer's time and gives them an opportunity to agree to listen.

You may also wish to outline exactly what you're going to cover during the call. Again, ask them if you can go over this information with them. This will show that you have given the phone call substantial thought, organized your information, and respect their time.

Asking Questions

Information gathering is an essential component of both incoming and outgoing telemarketing. Ask as many questions as possible and encourage your customer to start talking. This will keep you in control of the conversation. Even if these questions don't relate specifically to the product, your customer will provide firsthand information that you can add to your market research.

For incoming calls, listen to the customer's question, then ask if you can take a moment to ask them some questions before you answer theirs. This will allow you to explain your company's process, ask the customer some qualifying questions, and gain control of the conversation.

You will want to also consider asking questions related to the following topics:

- **Responsibility** – Who is in charge of making the decision? Is it the same person who will be making the purchase?
- **Budget** – How much financial resources are available for your product/service? What is the budget? What influences this number?
- **Timeframe** – When does the customer need the product or service? When will the transaction and delivery process have to be completed by? What is the reason for these deadlines?
- **Competition** – Who else is the customer talking to? What will impact their decision? What aspects are they comparing?

Closed-ended questions

Closed-ended questions are not the best way to get your customer talking, but they do provide information quickly and succinctly. Closed-ended questions are questions that can be answered with yes or no.

Open-ended questions

Open-ended questions are just that: they cannot be answered in one word. These are great questions to use for the majority of your telemarketing because they encourage the customer to provide explanations, giving you insight into their needs and opinions.

Obtaining Agreement

At key points throughout the conversation, you will need to ensure you are on the same page as your customer. You will need to find a way to get some feedback from your caller on what you have been saying.

An easy way to do this is to ask them a question you are sure they'll say yes to. Something like, "so as you can see, it's a pretty irresistible offer," or "I'm sure anyone would benefit from using these sprockets in their home."

Encouraging them to agree with you strengthens your argument and leads directly to the sale. It's a powerful method of persuasion.

Overcoming Objections

This will be the most challenging component of your script – largely because you do not know for sure what your customer's objections are going to be. You will have to think in the moment, and attempt to overcome each objection in a calm, professional way.

Before you pick up the phone, you may wish to brainstorm all potential objections, and think of your ideal response. A simple chart that looks like this will be a helpful tool to refer to during your call:

Potential Objection	Response

Remember to respect the objections as they are raised and treat each point your customer makes as a legitimate one. Show empathy and relate to what they have to say. Phrases like "I can see how that would be a concern for you…"

"I used to think the same thing…" and "Sure, that's completely understandable…" allow you to relate to them, establish common ground, and then share how you overcame your own objections.

Closing with Commitment

Once you have opened the conversation, developed a relationship, asked questions, secured agreement, and overcome objections, all you have to do is close the conversation with a commitment.

The commitment should be your objective for calling, or a step toward that objective. For example, if the purpose of your call was to set up a meeting, ensure that you commit to a time and place before you end the conversation. If your objective is to make a sale, you may have to make a few phone calls or hold a few appointments to achieve that.

Assume that if you have got this far, you have the sale. Be confident, and use phrases like, "How about we meet on this day at this time…" and "Where can I send the product?"

You will want to confirm whatever you have committed to in writing with your customer. If you have set an appointment, send them a quick note to thank them for the phone call, and put the meeting in writing. Remember to be as polite and succinct as possible. Avoid lengthy emails and letters.

Tips for Effective Telemarketing

Communicating with your existing and potential customers over the phone requires a different set of skills than in-person communication. Make sure you choose the best people for this job – when you only have your voice to communicate, you must be extra aware of the impression you give the person on the other line.

Smile

This may seem like a silly point to put at the top of this list, but it is important. Your caller will be able to hear if you are smiling and interpret your smile as enthusiasm. You will sound more positive, friendly, and open to dialogue. Remember, the person on the other line can hear *everything*, so avoid multi-tasking (drinking, eating, unnecessary typing) when you're on the phone.

Be a good listener

Once you get your customer talking – listen. They will be giving you important insight into their purchase motivations, and their potential objections. Take notes as you listen, and never assume you know what they are going to say. After long periods of speech, check in and repeat back what you have heard to confirm you have heard it properly. Make sure to leave a pause between what they have just said, and what you are about to say: showing that you have been listening.

Call at an optimal time

Knowing who you are calling will ensure that you contact them at the most appropriate time – the time they are most likely to answer you phone call. For example, business owners will need to be reached during business hours. Try to reach them during quiet times – usually first thing in the morning, or right before close. If you are calling consumers, then make your calls in the evening when they are most likely to be home.

Use a familiar tone

You only have your voice to establish a new relationship with a potential customer. The tone you choose is just as important – and has just as much impact – as the words you choose. Use a tone that is friendly and confident and resembles the way you would speak to your friends.

Be prepared to handle rejection

No matter how targeted your contact list, how amazing your script, how great your approach, rejection is an inevitable part of outgoing telemarketing. Your telemarketers are going to have to become very skilled at handling rejection. In fact, some people will not only reject what you have to say, they'll be rude in doing so. Remember not to take this personally – they could be having a bad day, or just not have enough time to listen to what you have to say. Consider asking to call back at a better time – or just shrug it off.

Be prepared to handle difficult customers

Difficult customers will appear on the other end of the phone line – for both incoming and outgoing calls. This is another inevitability of telemarketing, and business in general. Again, remember not to take what they have to say personally – they just want to air their frustrations and be heard. Listen intently, stay calm, and try to empathize with what they have to say. Never interrupt, use calming language, and record as much as possible about what they are saying. Then consider how you would like to handle the problem – try to resolve their issue immediately.

Make the call standing up

When you are standing, you will sound confident, authoritative, and decisive. Your diaphragm is expanded when you are standing, which will increase the confidence in your voice. Do this for the important phone calls – the big accounts.

Have strong phone manners

Here are some tips for ensuring you have a strong, professional phone presence:

- Ask for the contact by name, not role or title
- Use your full name when asked who is calling
- Clearly state your company name
- Tell them why you are calling
- If you do not reach your customer, ask for a more convenient time
- Do not hold, call back instead (your time is valuable, too!)

9

Double your Referrals

What if I told you that you could put an inexpensive system in place that would effectively allow your business to grow itself?

For most business owners, a large part of their customer base is comprised of referral customers. These people found out about the company's products or services from the recommendation of a friend or colleague who had a positive experience purchasing from that company.

If your business benefits from referral customers, you will find that these customers arrive ready to buy from you and tend to buy more often. They also tend to be highly loyal to your product or service.

Seem like great customers to have, don't they?

Referral customers cost less to acquire. Compared to the leads you generate from advertising, direct mail campaigns, and other marketing initiatives, referral customers come to you already qualified and already trusting in the quality of your offering and the respectability of your staff.

With a little effort, and the creation of a formalized system – or strategy – you can not only continue to enjoy referral business, but easily double the number of referral customers that walk through your door. All of this is possible for a minimal investment of time and resources.

Is Your Business a Referral Business?

Referral based businesses benefit from a stream of qualified customers who arrive at their doorstep ready to spend. These businesses put less focus on advertising to generate new leads, and more focus on serving and communicating with their existing customers.

Generally speaking, a referral program can generate outstanding results for nearly any business. Since most referrals do not require any effort, the addition of a strategy and a program will often double or triple the number of qualified referrals that come through a business door.

There are, however, a few types of businesses that will not benefit from a formalized referral strategy. These are businesses with low price points – like fast food restaurants and drugstores. Their customer base is large already, and their efforts would be best spent on increasing the average sale.

A referral program can:

- **Save you time**. Referral strategies – once established – don't require much management or time investment.
- **Deliver more qualified customers**. Your customer arrives with an assumption of trust, and willing to purchase.
- **Improve your reputation.** Your customer's networks likely overlap and create potential for a single customer to be referred by two people. This encourages the perception that your business is "the place to go."

- **Speed the sales process.** You will have existing common ground and a reputation with the referred customer.
- **Increase your profit.** You will spend less time and money generating leads, and more time serving customers who have their wallets open.

The Cost of Your Customers

As we discussed in the "Repeat Business" section, you don't "get" customers, you *buy* them. The money you spend on advertising, direct mail, and other promotions ideally results in potential customers walking through your doors.

For example, if you placed an ad for $200, and 20 people make a purchase in response to that ad, you would have paid $10 for each customer.

Referral customers cost you next to nothing. Your existing customer does the work of selling your business to their friend or associate, and you benefit from the sale. Aside from the cost of any referral incentives or coupon production, there is no cost involved at all.

Referral customers cost less and require less time investment than any other customer. That means you can spend that time making them a loyal customer, or a devoted fan.

Groom Your Customers

Referral strategies can allow you to groom your customer base. As we have previously discussed, 80% of your revenue comes from 20% of your customers – these are your ideal customers.

These are also the people you have established as your target market and are the people you cater your marketing and advertising efforts toward.

You also have a group of customers who make up 80% of your headaches. These are the people who complain the most and spend the least.

Use your referral strategy to get more of your *ideal* customers. Spend more time servicing your ideal customers – do everything you can to make them happy – and less time on your headache customers. You can even ask your headache customers to shop elsewhere.

Then, focus your referral efforts on your ideal customers. Ask them to refer business to you and reward them for doing so. Try to avoid referrals from your headache customers – chances are you'll just get another headache.

Referral Sources

Take some time to brainstorm all the people who could potentially refer business to you. Think beyond your business, to your extracurricular activities and personal life. There are endless sources of people who are ready and willing to send potential customers your way.

Here are some ideas to get you started:

Past Relationships

No, not romantic relationships. I'm talking about anyone you have previously had a relationship with, but for one reason or another have fallen out of touch. This includes former colleagues, associates, customers and friends.

Including them in your referral strategy can be as simple as reaching out through the phone or email, and updating them on your latest business initiative or career move. Gently ask at the end of the correspondence to refer anyone who may need your product or service. They will appreciate that you have attempted to re-establish the relationship.

Suppliers and Vendors

Your suppliers and vendors can be a great source for referrals, because they presumably deal daily with businesses that are complementary to your own. The opportunities to connect two of their customers in a mutually beneficial relationship are endless. These businesses should be happy to help out - especially if you have been a regular and loyal customer.

Customers

Customers are an obvious source of referrals because they are the people who are dealing with you directly on a regular basis. Often, all you have to do is ask and they will happily provide you with contact information of other interested buyers or contact those buyers themselves.

Your customers also have a high level of product knowledge when it comes to your business and are in a great position to really sell the strength of your company. Remember from the Testimonials section, the words of your customers are at least 10 times more powerful than any clever headline or marketing piece you could create.

Employees and Associates

Give your employees and associates a reason to have their friends and families shop at your business with a simple incentive program. These people have the most product knowledge and are in the best position to sell you to a potential customer.

This is also a way to tap into an endless network of people. Who do your employees and associates know? Who do their friends and friends of friends know? A referral chain that connects to your employees can be a highly powerful one.

Competitors

This doesn't seem so obvious, but it can work. Your direct competitors are clearly not the ideal source for referrals. However, indirect competitors can refer their clients or potential clients to you if they cannot meet those clients' needs themselves.

For example, if you sell high end lighting fixtures, the low-budget lighting store down the street may be able to refer clients to you, and vice versa. You may wish to offer a finder's fee or incentive to establish this arrangement.

Your Network

Don't be shy about asking your friends and family members for referrals. Too many people do not provide enough information to their inner circle about what they do or what their business does. This doesn't make sense, since these are the people who should be the most interested!

Take time to explain clearly what your business is all about, and what your point of difference is. Then just ask them if they know anyone who may benefit from what you are offering. You could even provide your friends and family with an incentive – a gift, a meal, or a portion of the sale.

Associations + Special Interest Groups

This is another place you likely have a network of people who have limited knowledge about what you do or what your business does. The advantage here is that you have a group of people with similar belief s and values in the same room. Use it!

The Media

Unless a member of the media is a regular customer of yours, or you are in business to serve the media, this may not seem like an obvious choice either.

The opportunity here is to establish a relationship with an editor or journalist and position yourself as an expert in your field or industry. Then, next time they are writing a related story, they can ask to quote you and your opinion. When their audience reads the story, they will perceive your business as the industry leader.

Referral Strategies

A referral strategy is any system you can put in place to generate new leads through existing customers. The ideal way to do this is to create a system that runs itself! Here are some ideas for simple strategies you can begin to implement into your business immediately.

Just Ask

This may seem simple and obvious, but it's true. Be open with your customers and associates, and simply ask them if they can refer any of their friends or associates to you. Make it part of doing business with you, and your customers will grow to expect the question. Or, let them know in advance that you'll be asking at a later date.

Remember that this can include potential customers – even if they don't buy from you. The reason they chose not to purchase may have nothing to do with your business; any person who has begun to or actually done business with you can refer to you another person.

Offer Incentives

When you speak to your customers, when you ask them for something, you typically try to answer the question "what's in it for me?" before they ask it.

The same is true when you ask your customers for a referral. Incentive-based referral strategies work wonders and can easily be implemented as part of a customer loyalty program, or as part of your existing customer relations systems.

Consider offering customers who successfully refer clients to you discounts on products, free products or services, or gifts. Offer incentives relative to the number of referrals, or the success rate of each referral.

This can have a spin off effect, as your referral customers may become motivated to continue the referral chain. They too will be interested in the incentives you have provided and tell their friends about your business.

Be Proactive

The only way your referral program will work is if you put some effort into it and maintain some level of ongoing effort.

Here are some ideas:

- Put a referral card or coupon in every shopping bag that leaves your store
- Promote gift certificates during peak seasons
- Offer free information seminars to existing customers, and ask them to bring a friend
- Host a closed-door sale for your top 20 customers and their friends

Provide Great Customer Service

An easy way to encourage referral business is to treat every potential customer with exemplary customer service. Since the art of customer service is lost is many communities, people are often impressed by simple added touches and conveniences. That alone will encourage them to refer your business to their network.

Stay in Touch

Make sure you are staying in touch with all of your potential and converted customers. Through newsletters, direct mail, or the Internet, keep your business name at the top of the minds, ahead of the competition.

Even if they have already purchased from you, and may not need to purchase for some time, a newsletter or email can be a simple reminder that your business is out there. If someone in their network is looking for the product or service, it will be more likely that your customer will refer your business over the competition.

10

Use Testimonials and Profit from Social Proof

The Power of Testimonials

Testimonials are simply the single most powerful asset you can have in your marketing toolkit. When your customers tell others about the benefits of choosing your business, it is a thousand times more powerful than the same words from your mouth.

The words and opinions of others motivate people to spend money every day. From celebrity endorsements on TV and in magazines, to casual conversations with friends, decisions about what product or service to buy – and what brand or provider – are heavily influenced by those who have purchased before.

Why? There are several reasons. Many people have an inherent distrust of salespeople, and a skepticism toward marketing materials. Others are bombarded with choice and are looking for some sense of security in their purchase decision.

Testimonials build the credibility of your business, break down natural barriers, and create a sense of trust for the consumer. They have an incredible ability to persuade customers to buy, and to buy from you. Think about the last time someone recommended a brand of laundry detergent, a bottle of wine, or a plumber to you. Their positive experience had more of an impact on your decision to buy than any advertisement or discount.

When it comes to spending money, people want a sure bet. They want to know that someone else has bought before, and they want to know that the product or service has delivered the promised results. A testimonial for your business is worth more than any copywriter, clever ad slogan, or sales pitch.

Customers Who Give Testimonials

When people put their name and reputation on paper to endorse something, it creates a sense of loyalty; if questioned, they will back their decision, even if they find later their decision was wrong.

When someone is willing to endorse your product or service in writing, they have likely already started a word-of-mouth chain of verbal testimonials about their positive experience. Remember the last time you discovered a chiropractic miracle worker? Or the fastest and cheapest drycleaner? Didn't you tell every one of your friends who could use the service?

By asking a customer for a testimonial, you are asking for their assistance in the growth of your business. When they feel they are truly helping and participating in the development of your company, their sense of pride will mean continuous loyalty to your product or service.

11 Ways to Get Great Testimonials

Testimonials are powerful – no question. But how do you make sure that the quotes you get from your customers will bring you the most value? How do you ensure that your client will articulate your product's merits in a clear and easy to understand way? How do you make sure you can actually use their testimonials in your marketing materials?

Asking for testimonials requires more effort than merely soliciting general comments and praise. You want to ensure that your customer feels a sense of pride and loyalty in providing their opinion, and that their opinion will have an impact on potential buyers.

How? Glad you asked. Here are 11 proven ways to get great testimonials from your customers.

1. Don't wait!

Your customers are the happiest and most willing to help you within a day to a week of their purchase, so aim to secure the testimonial in this time period. Ask for the testimonial before they leave, and make sure you have all their contact details to follow up with. This also ensures you stay on top of your testimonial recruitment!

2. Get specific

Specific testimonials are more believable. The more specific you can have your customer be, the stronger and more impactful the testimonial will be. Remember the Sleep Country testimonials that referenced the little "booties" that their delivery men wore to keep carpets clean? Meaningful details get remembered. Ask for mention of things like time, dates, extraordinary customer service, and personal observations.

3. If you were the solution – what was the problem?

Testimonials that tell stories are more engaging. Ask client to not only describe their experience with your company, but also the negative experience that led them to your door. If they can describe the struggles and challenges they were facing before receiving your service, the reader will likely be able to sympathize and resonate with similar struggles. This will motivate them to solve their problems with your solution.

4. Write the first draft

Make it easy for your clients. This technique is something you can offer someone who is hesitant to commit to writing a testimonial due to time constraints or is procrastinating. Ask them to brainstorm a few notes they would like to include in their feedback, write them down, and string them into a concise testimonial for their review. All they have to do is review, print on their letterhead, sign, and mail back to you!

5. Include your marketing message or USP

Always ask your customers to include your unique selling proposition (USP) in the testimonial. For instance, if your USP includes exceptional customer service, same-day installation, and a money-back guarantee then ask your customer to attest to those qualities.

6. A picture says…

Yes, you know the saying. But it's true. When readers attach an image of the speaker to words, the words are enlivened and have twice as much validity and impact. When readers see an image of a previous client using your product or service, their words and opinions are even more believable. You can take these simple pictures yourself – and take many so you have a selection to choose from.

7. Credentials equal trust

As we mentioned, testimonials from credible sources will have the most believability and impact. When you ask for a testimonial, make sure your customer states their expertise and credentials. If you sell custom orthotics, and can secure a solid testimonial from a doctor, their words will be golden in your marketing materials.

8. Don't forget to ask permission

When you ask for testimonials, make sure you are clear that their words may be used in your marketing materials, including advertisements, website and in-store displays. This is a good time to thank them for their time and sincerity and show your appreciation for their words.

9. Location, location…

Depending on the market reach of your business, the location of your customers is an important part of the believability of your testimonial. If you own a community-based business, when potential clients see you've made others happy just down their street they'll be motivated to use your service too.

If you own a regional business, then the cities and addresses of other happy customers can help communicate the reach of your service.

10. Testimonials are not surveys

Keep the purpose of your request in mind when you're asking for testimonials. Testimonials should be positive fodder for your advertising materials. Surveys are used to solicit meaningful (and often confidential) customer information to refine and improve your service. Testimonials are public statements, while surveys are often anonymous and can produce less-than-positive results.

11. Say thank you!

Thanking a customer for their time and effort creating your testimonial is just plain good manners. It also increases loyalty and goodwill. This can be done via email but sending a formal letter on your letterhead is a more meaningful approach.

Using Testimonials Strategically

So now you have a pile of glowing customer testimonials. What's next?

Choose the most powerful piece of the testimonial

What is the most convincing aspect of the testimonial? Is it the author? Where they are from? A specific sentence or paragraph they wrote? Be strategic about the aspect of the testimonial that you feature and select what will have the most impact.

For example, you can compile a list titled *What Customers are Saying*, and list only the phrases that support your specific marketing message. Or you can feature the unique credentials or story of your customer, before you even include their testimonial. You can also summarize the testimonial with a powerful headline.

Put them on your website

Adding a page of testimonials to your website is a great start, especially when you're beginning to solicit customer responses. However, the most powerful way to ensure site visitors actually see your testimonials is to include them on every page – especially the ones with the highest traffic.

A testimonial should be placed wherever you make a strong statement about your service or product, and wherever the service or product is described. This is a great way to break up your sales copy with some "proof". As they read about your offering, your credibility will be validated by someone other than you.

Compile your best 25 to 50 letters in a display book

Like a proud grandparent, keep a book of testimonials in the waiting area of your office, your boardroom, and in your desk. Or, put one at the service counter, cash register and anywhere else people may have a moment to flip through.

I've seen this done in recruiting firm, a hardware store, and a physiotherapist's office. When clients have a chance to read the positive experiences of others, they will be more open to hearing your sales pitch less guarded when responding to your unique offering.

Hang your favorite testimonials in your store or office

Testimonials as art! Frame your favorite testimonials – preferably the ones written on client letterhead – and post them on the wall in your business. Even if clients don't read them up close, the volume and visual recognition of client logos will have impact. Plus – your next satisfied clients will want to see their company names on the wall too.

Put them in your advertisements

Use short, clear, concise testimonials in your advertising. When was the last time you saw a prescription drug advertisement without a testimonial? Can't remember? That's because you haven't. The best advertisers know that testimonials are the fastest and most effective way to overcome skepticism and get clients thinking that your product or service is the solution to their problem.

Include a page of testimonials in your direct mail

When sending your marketing materials directly to a mass list of potential clients, let the words of others speak to the merits of your product or service. Put together a page or two of testimonials and attach it to your mailing. The credibility of your company will be instantly established, encouraging clients to act – and buy – faster.

Partner with an associate for joint mailing

If you have an associate or colleague who has a similar customer base of new prospects for your business, try a joint-endorsed mailing. Each of you will send a letter to your own clients, endorsing the other's products and services. Your service or solution is offered to a potential client by a trusted source, and you are offering your existing clients the added value of an associate's service to complement your own.

Testimonial Request Letter

Here is an example of a basic testimonial request letter that can be customized and made into a template for your unique business. This can also be sent over email if that is how your clients prefer to be contacted.

Mr. John Smith
1234 Main Street
Anytown, Anyplace 90210

January 2, 2006

Dear Mr. Smith,

Thank you for visiting our store this week. It was a pleasure helping you select a new laptop for your daughter to use at university this fall – they just grow up too fast! Your research and clear idea of the product you were searching for truly made our job easy. We love the back to school season, because it means working with clients like yourself.

We know there are a lot of choices when it comes to purchasing a laptop in Anytown, so thank you for choosing ABC Company. If there is anything else we can assist you with, please don't hesitate to contact me directly.

We occasionally ask select customers for their feedback in the form of a testimonial. Because we are so proud of the feedback we receive, we often use our customer's quotes in our marketing materials – specifically our website and sales brochures. The real-life experiences of our customers at ABC Company are stories that we are proud of.

Could I ask you to write down some of your feedback? A few words about your experience with ABC Company, and how we helped you and your daughter would be greatly appreciated. We encourage you to print this on your company letterhead, so we can provide your own company with some exposure as well.

You may want to include the names of the associates who helped you, and how your daughter is enjoying her laptop. Again, we would like to feature your name and experience in our marketing materials. For your convenience, I've included a prepaid envelope with which to mail your testimonial back to us.

Thank you very much for your assistance.

Kind regards,

Your name here

Testimonial Thank You Letter

Here is an example of a short thank you letter for a testimonial that can also be customized and made into a template for your unique business. You may wish to write your thank you letters on company note cards, but try to avoid sending these thank you's via email.

Mr. John Smith
1234 Main Street
Anytown, Anyplace 90210

January 10, 2006

Dear Mr. Smith,

We received your glowing testimonial in the mail today, and I wanted to thank you personally for your kind words. Your comments about our store and our people are important to us, and I will make sure my staff takes a moment to read your letter.

We are thrilled that your daughter is enjoying her laptop and using it to keep in touch with you while she studies abroad. When we sold it to you, we truly believed it would provide the most long-lasting value for her student budget. I hope it serves her for the rest of her time at school.

Thank you again for taking the time to write us. We are all proud to have been of service to you and your daughter and look forward to seeing you both again soon.

Warm regards,

Your Name Here

Testimonial Examples

Below you will find a series of sample testimonials, and excerpts from testimonial letters. Read these over and take a moment to notice why each is a powerful statement. We have also summarized each testimonial with a headline.

24% Response Rate from a Single Direct Mailing!

We were skeptical about direct mail campaigns, and unsure about the return on investment. Your strategic advice and logistical help made the project run smoothly and easily – we received over 200 leads from this single effort!
John and Betty McFee
Scottsdale, AZ

Best Sleep in 20 Years!

I can't tell you how much I appreciated Craig's patience and assistance in my mattress selection. He is so knowledgeable of each mattress' design and features and helped us find a financing solution that worked with our budget. I haven't slept this well in over two decades. Promote him!
  Jason Carmichael

Gentle and effective approach

I have always been reluctant to visit a chiropractor for my lower back pain because I am not comfortable with physical adjustments. Sarah took the time to clearly explain the cause of my pain and gave me easy exercises to help correct the problem. She respected my comfort level and treated me without uncomfortable cracks and snaps!
Wally Orton

Testimonial Worksheet

Start today! Brainstorm a list of recent customers and clients who you will approach for testimonials. Post this worksheet in your office and track your progress. Aim for 50 testimonials in two months. You can never have too many.

Name + Phone	Request Letter Sent	Follow Up Call Made	Testimonial Received	Thank-you Letter Sent
	☐	☐	☐	☐
	☐	☐	☐	☐
	☐	☐	☐	☐
	☐	☐	☐	☐
	☐	☐	☐	☐
	☐	☐	☐	☐
	☐	☐	☐	☐
	☐	☐	☐	☐
	☐	☐	☐	☐
	☐	☐	☐	☐
	☐	☐	☐	☐
	☐	☐	☐	☐
	☐	☐	☐	☐
	☐	☐	☐	☐
	☐	☐	☐	☐
	☐	☐	☐	☐
	☐	☐	☐	☐
	☐	☐	☐	☐

So What Do You Do From Here?

Hopefully you have quite a bit of notes and ideas on how to proceed. You may have a lot of questions. This is all good. You may even already have a "business plan" or "marketing plan" or "product plan" developed. Remember to take your ideas and sound them out with your customers.

One last lesson. So where do you go from here?

Measure twice and cut once: Fail Fast!

The faster you fail, the less money and time you will lose and the more profit you will receive. Don't sacrifice the good for the perfect--maintain your quality, but many customers will happily help you develop your business-- remember they want you to succeed. They want you to provide them with the services and products that they want and need. They will even pay you for them.

Find out what they value from you and then give it to them. Talk to customers and see what they think you could do to build a better business? Offer to talk to former customers and listen to what they tell you. Even if you lost them because what you did was "right," they may have something to teach you.

Of course, some people cannot be pleased, some people are outrageous, and some people are just plain unfair; but, even listening to those individuals can teach you something that may give you an edge for the people with whom you do want to partner with as your customer.

Planning a successful business/product is predicated on the following four components: Product Development, Messaging, Sales Tactics, Product Delivery.

Test as you are planning. Test as you execute. Don't' stop testing even when you have found success.

Finally, always keep your idea on the fundamental formula powering your Sky-High Profit Rocket:

$$\text{Customer's Wants} + \text{Needs} = \text{Your Customer's Problem}$$
$$\text{Customer's Problem} - \text{Your Solution} = \text{Your Revenue}$$
$$\text{Your Revenue} - \text{Your Costs} = \text{Your Profit}$$

For additional resources please visit us at:

www.The-Business-Toolbox.com